**U.S. Department
of Transportation**

SURFACE TRANSPORTATION VULNERABILITY ASSESSMENT

General Distribution Version

**FINAL REPORT
October 25, 2001**

**Research and Special Programs Administration
John A. Volpe National Transportation Systems Center
and
Office of Intelligence and Security
Office of the Secretary**

Preface

This document is a partial reprint of the Surface Transportation Vulnerability Assessment dated February 26, 1999. This version has been edited to allow for general distribution. This document was originally written prior to the September 11, 2001 incidents, and did not focus on countermeasures for or impacts of use of transportation assets as a means of threat delivery.

Table of Contents

List of Figures

List of Tables

EXECUTIVE SUMMARY

The United States possesses an effective and efficient surface transportation infrastructure that promotes both the well-being of its citizens as well as important economic and national security goals. The level of security afforded this infrastructure is relatively low compared to the security enhancements recently implemented in the commercial aviation sector. However, there is sufficient reason to believe that the security levels of the surface transportation modes need to be raised as the threat level increases and the vulnerabilities of the current infrastructure become apparent. There are potential threat scenarios where a significant loss of human life or a major disruption to a key segment of the nation's transportation infrastructure could occur. Given this fact, it is essential that well-planned, coordinated actions be taken to reduce the possibility that such events occur. Such actions should represent a coordinated approach by a partnership of public and private sector institutions to: identify vulnerabilities and threats; and enhance the security of key surface transportation infrastructure segments and operations.

Objectives

The national transportation system of the United States consists of interconnected infrastructures including highways, transit systems, railroads, airports, waterways, pipelines and ports, as well as the vehicles, aircraft and vessels that operate along these networks. This system also includes the industries, companies, and public and private sector organizations that make these activities possible. It is undisputed that the effective operation of this system is essential to the continued prosperity, quality of life, economic productivity and competitiveness, and national security of the nation and its citizens.

However, both national and international trends have given rise to concerns about the safety and security of this system and its key components should they be targeted by an adversary, and about the impact of degradations to this system. Recent events such as the sarin nerve gas incidents in Japanese subway stations and the bombings of the World Trade Center, Atlanta's Olympic Park and the Oklahoma City Federal building within the U.S. have given many people pause to consider the security of major public environments. This concern is reflected in such recent reports as the White House Commission on Aviation Safety and Security, and the Presidential Commission on Critical Infrastructure Protection (PCCIP).

Thus, this is an appropriate time to build upon these and related studies and undertake an analysis of the vulnerability of the national surface transportation system to such threats. In fact, the FY 1996 Department of Transportation supplemental appropriation authorized and funded the Surface Transportation Vulnerability Assessment Program (VAP) for this purpose. This activity is managed within the Department by the Research and Special Programs Administration (RSPA), with advice from the Office of Intelligence and Security (S-60) within the Office of the Secretary of Transportation (OST).

This "Surface Transportation Vulnerability Assessment" report is the major product of this VAP initiative. This analysis includes consideration of several key factors. It identifies the major threats to surface transportation. It describes and assesses the vulnerability of key transportation elements and the potential impact of attacks on them. It summarizes the current and future countermeasures that can most effectively mitigate these impacts. Finally, in light of this information, it recommends a series of improvements that can be made to enhance the overall safety and security of the surface transportation system.

Scope and Method

This assessment provides the framework and methodology to assist in making informed decisions to mitigate identified surface transportation vulnerabilities. It focuses on the five major surface transportation modes: highway; maritime; pipeline; rail; and public transit; as well as intermodal freight and passenger transportation. For purposes of this report, 'threats' consist of potential deliberate actions by an adversary or criminal that could degrade important segments of the national transportation system. Such threats include the use of explosives or Weapons of Mass Destruction (WMD), sabotage, acts of violence, and 'cyber' attacks targeting key computer and information systems supporting transportation operations. This latter threat is of increasing concern, given the rapidly growing reliance of modern transportation on technological systems and tools.

A vulnerability / impact analysis methodology is presented to assess the vulnerability of individual transportation elements and the potential impact of a successful attack on them. The process is based on developing scenarios in which threat events occur in individual instances, assessing the vulnerabilities to these threats, evaluating the negative consequences - or impacts - of these events, and identifying and recommending potential countermeasures.

When this process is completed, it is possible to develop a priority listing of these vulnerabilities, based on calculations of the criticality of the impacts of these events, as well as suggestions for appropriate countermeasures.

For purposes of this analysis, it was assumed that the attack in each scenario does occur – thus, what is being assessed is *the likelihood of significant consequences, of an attack.* Before appropriate decisions on countermeasures and resource allocation can be made, it is important to determine the *likelihood that a particular attack would occur,* based on accurate threat information. That assessment was not conducted as part of this effort.

Conclusions: Surface Transportation Vulnerabilities and Potential Impact of Attacks

There are several important generalizations that can be drawn about scenarios, vulnerabilities, and impacts for the individual transportation modes.

Current Security Levels

None of these surface transportation modes currently exhibit a substantial security or anti-terrorism profile, particularly when compared to the emphasis commercial aviation places on these activities. The primary reason for this situation is historical: in the U.S. experience, aviation, particularly in an overseas environment, has been by far the most visible and dramatic transportation target for terrorism and violent criminal incidents. Few similar actual incidents involving domestic surface transportation assets have occurred. Thus, each mode has responded to its own specific security and terrorist history, and has developed and implemented security practices that are consistent with its actual and assessed vulnerabilities. It is not surprising, then, that the likelihood of a successful threat event is judged to be so high in most of the scenarios. There are, in fact, few examples of sustained or resource-intensive security practices in surface transportation, due to the absence of firm justification for such an approach to date. In addition, the open nature of the surface transportation environment makes it difficult, if not impractical, to apply security measures that would hinder the movements of individuals. However, the indisputable increase in the potential threat to these facilities in recent years is reason to review this situation and point out potential areas of concern.

Vulnerabilities and Impacts

Many surface transportation assets are very vulnerable to potential attack. Those scenarios judged as possessing 'catastrophic' impacts tend to represent situations where large numbers of people are affected by explosives or chemical/biological toxins, or where a key infrastructure element, such as a major bridge, tunnel or dock, is damaged or destroyed by a large explosive force. These situations include large, public passenger terminals, or specific infrastructure segments whose loss would have the most serious impacts on traffic patterns and the economy. Those scenarios judged to have a 'very serious' impacts include smaller explosives causing damage to individual infrastructure elements which would cause significant traffic and economic impacts but which could be more readily repaired or rectified. Finally, those scenarios with

'moderate' impacts deal with individual violent criminal acts, such as shootings, as well as disruptions to information and communications systems by 'cyber' attacks.

These findings suggest that the most attention and resources should be devoted to the 'catastrophic' situations first, followed by the latter two categories, so that the most harmful and disruptive impacts would receive the highest priority. It should again be noted, however, that an assessment of the likelihood that a particular transportation facility or operation would be targeted in this manner should also be a part of the decision-making process on resource allocations.

The relatively low level of impacts on transportation predicted from 'cyber' incidents is not surprising. Few surface transportation operations are presently so dependent on information or communications systems that their disruption would cause serious consequences. This situation can be expected to change in the future, however, as these technologies become increasingly important to support transportation operations. In the case of Intelligent Transportation Systems (ITS), for example, no region has yet implemented a full-scale ITS operation in which an integrated set of these technologies is actually significantly affecting a large number of driver decisions or traffic patterns. Within five to ten years, however, a number of regions plan to have fully implemented the Intelligent Transportation Infrastructure (ITI) package of at least seven major user services including transit, traffic and incident management capabilities. The impact on these regions of losing these services will be significantly higher than at present.

Modal Variations

This study assessed the vulnerability of the critical components of the individual surface transportation modes. However, in reviewing the vulnerabilities and impacts, it is apparent that each mode presents a somewhat different picture.

Highways represent both the most important single surface mode - when looking at the total volume of passengers and freight together - and also the most robust and resilient mode. By its status as the most extensive physical infrastructure, this mode has by far the largest number of alternative routes which, with varying levels of inconvenience, can be used to redirect high-priority traffic. The most vulnerable segments of this network appear to be bridges and tunnels, due to their accessibility, the expense and difficulty of replacing them, and their concentration of several routes into a single infrastructure segment. Successful attacks on bridges or tunnels could impact many people who depend on such structures for both passenger and freight movements.

In the case of public transit, the operating region of each major service provider is restricted to a single urban area. Thus, the direct impact of an attack on a single system would be limited geographically to that urban area. There may be limited impacts outside of that area if the site handles major connections between modes or long-distance lines. This would be the case if, for example, an incident involving the Chicago transit system were to affect the ability of large numbers of travelers to make their onward Amtrak or commercial aviation connections. It is also important to note that the impact on the affected area itself may be quite severe and require Federal assistance. The loss of mass transit in New York City for a sustained period of time, for example, could cause significant local travel delays, impede the forwarding of key cargoes, and have major negative economic impacts on the nation as a whole. In addition, public transit incidents also have the potential for affecting the largest number of passengers and having the largest number of casualties.

In the case of rail, maritime, pipeline, and intermodal freight, the smaller extent of the networks tends to limit the choice of effective alternate routes to a destination. In some circumstances, shifting to an alternate mode may not be feasible in the short term, due to the characteristics of the cargo itself or the physical absence of a practical alternative. As with highways, they tend to possess infrastructure elements that are particularly vulnerable. These include rail bridges and tunnels, and maritime dock and port facilities.

Impacts of Technology on Vulnerabilities

In each mode, albeit to varying degrees, advanced technologies are increasingly being applied to improve the operational performance and overall management of transportation activities. Every mode is employing the Global Positioning System (GPS) satellite constellation for position location, real-time tracking, navigation, or mapping applications. Modern telecommunications is becoming the backbone for traffic management systems. Electronic Data Interchange (EDI) of cargo shipment information is essential for competitive freight service. ITS technologies are becoming commonplace in highway and public transit settings. Supervisory Control and Data Acquisition (SCADA) systems are managing large-scale pipeline networks.

It is important to remember, however, that each of these technological applications also brings with it a corresponding new or increased vulnerability. Reliance on GPS requires that satellite signals be received and processed accurately. If this capability were lost, it may be difficult to compensate readily by turning to another backup navigation system or by relying on other non-technological aids. In a similar manner, losing or receiving inaccurate EDI information could complicate freight routing and delivery. When ITS technologies are more extensively deployed, their sudden loss or degradation could have a similar impact on highway congestion and public transit services. This could be particularly painful for the trucking industry, which is concerned about including proprietary data in the implementation of the national ITS Commercial Vehicle Operations (CVO) user service.

Impacts of Other Developments

Other improvements to the efficiency of transportation operations may also impact vulnerabilities. The deregulation of major transportation sectors in the 1970s, combined with the introduction of new manufacturing and logistics techniques (lean manufacturing, just-in-time delivery) and the consolidation of service providers into fewer but larger firms, has undoubtedly improved the performance of the transportation sector and brought significant time and cost savings to users. However, these improvements have acted to 'squeeze out' excess and underutilized capacity from the transportation system. Many rail lines have been abandoned or are non-operational. The traffic level on key infrastructure segments has approached or even exceeded capacity under normal circumstances, and congestion and travel delays are already increasing.

The consequence of this development is that the current level of daily operations are closer to total capacity and, in fact, the application of technologies such as ITS can lead to traffic volumes that are greater than the physical infrastructure by itself can manage. This actually makes it easier to create system-wide 'gridlock' by degrading the technological application. Thus, even though the overall transportation system is operating normally at a higher level of efficiency, it has also lost a significant amount of the inherent 'robustness' and flexibility that existed when excess route capacity could absorb sudden increases in

demand or act as detours on short notice when required.

This situation is further compounded by the military's reliance on commercial transportation. As the Department of Defense has 'down-sized' and sought more cost-effective operations, it is turning to available commercial assets to meet its transportation and logistics requirements in peacetime, wartime, and in case of national emergencies. If a series of successful attacks in these key infrastructure elements were to occur at the same time as a major military mobilization, the consequences could be severe.

Finally, there have been concerns expressed by some observers about the overall current status of the nation's physical infrastructure. A number of DOT reports, for example, suggest that large numbers of the nation's bridges and major segments of the highway and rail network are obsolete or deficient and require immediate rehabilitation or replacement. This situation can have serious consequences in the event of attacks on this system. A structurally defective bridge, for example, would require even less explosives to collapse than would a bridge in good condition. Thus, the poor condition of a target itself may magnify the impact of an attack.

Recommendations for Action

This report by itself does not provide all relevant information needed to make decisions on allocating security resources among surface transportation elements. For that to occur, it would also be necessary to assess the likelihood that individual segments would be targeted by an adversary. In the interim, however, there are a number of important conclusions that can be drawn.

First, it is evident that terrorism presents a threat to the nation itself, and not solely to any single element of transportation. Thus, protecting key transportation assets from this threat should be an issue of national importance, and not one solely for the transportation sector to resolve. In addition, since transportation itself directly involves a range of participants across society, the response to this threat should represent a coordinated effort by a partnership of the concerned public and private sector institutions and individuals. Although terrorism is a national concern, security is first and foremost a responsibility of the service provider. Many steps taken by operators to improve security against common criminals contribute to deterring terrorists.

As one of the most important participants in this sector of national life, the Federal government has a key role in this entire effort. Its responsibilities should include:

- facilitating high-priority projects and promising research and development of security enhancements

- helping to coordinate and improve data collection and analysis, and threat assessment and warning activities

- participating in the development and dissemination of security-related standards, guidelines, manuals, procedures and policies

- coordinating an industry-wide education program to heighten awareness of security issues among transportation operators and clients

Topics such as chemical/biological threats and responses, information systems security, and improved perimeter security and access control methods should receive particular attention.

There are a wide range of protective features and prudent precautions that can be taken to diminish the chances that a successful attack on a segment of the transportation system would occur. In the context of this report, these actions are termed *countermeasures*. These countermeasures are often applicable - given appropriate modification - in one form or another to similar situations in every mode and location. A number of these responses can be implemented quickly at a very low or negligible cost; in fact, they should probably already be part of day-to-day operational and administrative practices because of the inherent benefits that they bring even in normal circumstances. Other countermeasures may require significant time and effort to put into place, but may represent the best choice for assuring the continued functioning of a key transportation operation under all but the most determined assault. Even then, however, it is important to recognize that it is virtually impossible to guarantee the integrity of any target if it is attacked by a determined adversary with the necessary resources and the willingness to employ them. Thus, it is best to see these countermeasures as ways to minimize the potential for such a successful high-impact assault under all but the most extreme conditions, rather than as a 'complete' solution.

There are three major categories of countermeasures that can be applied to transportation situations. They are:

- defining problems
- developing solutions
- implementing these solutions in daily operations.

Defining Problems

Under the first category, individual risk assessments of key transportation facilities and operations should be performed, so that their specific vulnerabilities and needs can be assessed. Timely and accurate threat information is also a primary prerequisite for any meaningful countermeasures strategy. Without this capability it is difficult, if not impossible, to gauge the extent or nature of the threat, assess the major vulnerabilities, disseminate warnings, and choose the most effective responses. A common information-based requirement is creation of a comprehensive and updated database of basic threat information and processes to analyze this data and assess possible threats. It is essential that the products of the analysis are accessible by the operators and managers of transportation activities. Important security-related information on existing transportation infrastructure assets can be added to current databases. In addition, improvements can be made in the current capabilities for rapidly assessing threat-related information and notifying responsible parties of the existence and nature of a credible threat, so that planned responses can be initiated before an incident occurs. Freedom of Information Act (FOIA) requirements should be taken into consideration in design and development of any comprehensive or sensitive database.

Developing Effective Solutions

Of equal importance to defining the problem and obtaining and assessing information about threats and vulnerabilities is the second countermeasure category: developing effective solutions - or *countermeasures* - to these problems. Common standards and guidelines for effective security strategies should be developed as part of a consolidated effort involving both public and private sector organizations. A major input for this process should be best practice surveys of transportation operators and managers, in which the characteristics of the most effective security operations can be publicized to others in the community. In addition, one of the primary sources for

current and potential future countermeasure solutions is in the development and application of key technologies. This will grow even further in importance as advances in materials, information, telecommunications and other fields continue to be applied to improving transportation operations. Supporting additional research into technological applications to countermeasures can bring real benefits for a number of users. Among the specific areas in which these developments can be helpful are:

- using advanced materials and new designs to improve the resistance of key infrastructure elements (such as tunnels and bridge supports) to blast effects

- improved sensors for toxins, weapons and explosives detection

- non-intrusive inspection methods for cargo and containers

- improved access control, monitoring, secure communications equipment, and information systems security

Prototype demonstrations of these new products can be conducted and the results made available to the wider community. As with the other countermeasure categories, these activities can be most successfully pursued as joint efforts involving government and industry representatives from all transportation modes and areas.

Implementing these Solutions

Finally, the ultimate goal of any security enhancement effort is the actual implementation of effective countermeasures in the transportation community. Depending on the results of the risk assessments, immediate low-cost improvements can be implemented at individual sites:

- adding physical barriers such as fences, gates and bollards

- increasing surveillance and monitoring equipment and security personnel

- implementing effective security-related practices and procedures

In the wider context, government and industry should work together to: implement and enforce effective security procedures; assign responsibility for security-related activities to the appropriate parties; and develop and test effective emergency response and restoration of service plans. Again, these actions are best undertaken in a coordinated framework within all modes and by every major organization with operational, managerial and emergency response responsibilities for transportation.

In the event of safety or security threat of the transportation system, the Secretary of Transportation has extensive authority over all air and water transportation and limited authority over any other mode of transportation. The Secretary of Transportation also has extensive authority to organize all modes of transportation to aid in rescue or evacuation in case of an emergency. In time of war, the President, acting through the Secretary of Defense, can take control of all or any part of the transportation system of the United States to deal with the emergency.

Finally, assuring the overall reduction in transportation vulnerabilities requires a large-scale and coordinated education and training approach. The customers of this effort are the operators, managers and users of transportation services and facilities. Stressing the need for employee and customer awareness and vigilance has been shown to be a very effective and important element in security strategies. Informing and involving the public as partners in identifying security problems and minimizing the impact of their occurrence can be as valuable as training transportation workers in these skills.

Such programs could include:

- developing and distributing guidelines, handbooks, training materials, and presentations of 'best practices' examples of effective countermeasures programs in real organizations

- offering workshops, symposia and training courses on specific topics

- incorporating such materials into the formal transportation, logistics and security-related curricula in technical schools, colleges and universities

This should be considered an important continuous activity: new employees are constantly entering the transportation work force, and new threat information, technologies, procedures and methods are constantly becoming available. Thus, ongoing education and training in security and countermeasures should become an integral part of a lifetime learning program for all transportation employees and users.

INTRODUCTION 1

As part of the FY 1996 supplemental appropriations bill, funds were provided to the U.S. Department of Transportation (DOT) to support a comprehensive Surface Transportation Vulnerability Assessment Program (VAP). The VAP is funded and managed by the Department's Research and Special Programs Administration (RSPA) with advice from the Office of Intelligence and Security (OIS). In addition, the National Academy of Sciences (NAS) will form an Advisory Committee on Surface Transportation Security, composed of technical and policy experts, who will assist DOT with this effort. This Committee will identify promising policies, procedures, organizational changes, and technology applications that could improve the security of surface transportation modes, and it will recommend areas of technology or operations that should be further researched, developed, tested and evaluated to improve surface transportation security.

This report, based on the VAP findings, identifies critical surface transportation system assets and likely threat scenarios. It rates the degrees of difficulty of attacking these assets successfully and the resulting impacts. Furthermore, recommendations for preventing or mitigating such attacks are presented.

Background

The U.S. transportation system is comprised of an integrated network of public roads, navigable waterways and ports, railroads, bus and rail transit systems, airports, and pipelines. Passengers, cargo, and information are transferred throughout the country on the infrastructure and in the vehicles that serve this system, reaching major population centers, smaller cities, and remote areas. In 1994 alone, the domestic transportation system accommodated more than 4.2 trillion passenger-miles of travel, and 3.7 trillion ton-miles of freight[1]. As users continually require faster and more extensive service, the transportation network's efficiency, complexity, and inter-connectivity have grown. Transportation providers and facilities are implementing new information technologies and logistics practices responsive to changing business environments.

Program Approach

The VAP builds on other studies, projects, and efforts that have been performed by DOT and by other federal agencies and, most notably the following:

- The *President's Commission on Critical Infrastructure Protection (PCCIP)*

- The *Infrastructure Protection Task Force*

- The *Interagency Information Infrastructure Planning Team* of the National Science and Technology Committee's (NSTC's) *Transportation R&D Coordinating Committee*

- The *National Security Telecommunications Advisory Committee (NSTAC)*

- The *White House Commission on Aviation Safety and Security*

- The *Department of Defense's Infrastructure Assurance Program (IAP)*

- The *Naval Surface Warfare Center Joint Program Office (JPO) for Special Technology Countermeasures*

The program approach provides comprehensive coverage of the national transportation

---

[1]   U.S. Department of Transportation, Bureau of Transportation Statistics, *Transportation Statistics Annual Report 1995* (Washington, DC: 1995), p. 3.

infrastructure in both *passenger* and *freight* modes and was designed to meet the following objectives:

- To evaluate and prioritize the vulnerability of the nation's transportation system to identified threats

- To identify potential countermeasures and best practices for the mitigation of key vulnerabilities

- To better posture DOT to manage the changing threat environment

Scope and Assumptions

Nature of Study

The purpose of the effort was to assess the likelihood of a loss given an attack, the impact of that loss, and to make recommendations that will decrease the likelihood and reduce the impact of such attacks on the component of the surface transportation modes. *However, the probability of an attack being made is not addressed.* Instead, the likelihood of loss assumes that a perpetrator with means and intent launches an attack. The impact of loss assumes that the attack was fully successful.

Modes Under Study

Five modes of transportation make up the U.S. surface transportation system:

- Highway
- Maritime
- Pipeline
- Public Transit
- Rail

This study also includes intermodal transfer facilities and intermodal cargo. Several modes provide both freight and passenger service. For example, rail passenger transport (Amtrak and commuter) is conducted on tracks that also transport freight. Each mode, and its corresponding freight and passenger service,

will be discussed individually in subsequent chapters.

Threats

This report focuses on *vulnerabilities* to a fixed set of *threats*. Each of these threats presents the potential to impact, to varying degrees, the operation of transportation systems and to cause harm to humans. This report deals with acts of terrorism, including sabotage, and acts of extreme violence as part of a terrorist agenda. It does not include such threats as natural disasters, accidents, and crime.

Terrorist threats can be carried out using several modes of attack/weapons - use of explosives, release of chemical or biological agents, exploitation of information or communication systems, and conventional arms. Chapter 3 discusses these threats in greater detail.

Information Security Statement

This report focused primarily on physical vulnerability to surface transportation security rather than cyber issues, with some exceptions. Cyber issues that were addressed include remote signaling for rail and pipeline (SCADA), intelligent transportation systems, and the vulnerability of commercial vehicle electronic data interchange. Focusing the report in this way was done intentionally as it was completed concurrently to the work of the President's Commission on Critical Infrastructure Protection (PCCIP).

Historically, many of the nation's critical infrastructures have been physically and logically separate systems that had little interdependence. As a result of advances in information technology and the necessity of improved efficiency, however, these infrastructures have become increasingly automated and interlinked. These same advances have created new vulnerabilities to equipment failures, human error, weather and other natural causes and physical and cyber attacks. The PCCIP's objective was to understand these threats to and vulnerabilities of the nation's critical infrastructure, with a particular focus on information security. Critical infrastructures were defined as those physical and cyber-based systems essential to the minimum operations of the economy and government. They include, but are not limited to telecommunications, energy, banking and finance, water systems, emergency services, and transportation, both government and private.

With the exception of the National Airspace System and the St. Lawrence Seaway, the private sector or state and local agencies own and operate the nation's transportation infrastructure. As a result, DOT has previously assumed little responsibility for protecting and critical transportation infrastructure, with the exception of civil aviation security, cruise and ship port security, and the safe transportation of hazardous materials (see *Appendix E – Authority of the Secretary of Transportation in Emergencies*). The transportation section of the PCCIP report addresses cyber vulnerabilities relating to all modes of transportation, particularly those affecting the National Airspace System. The report also concentrates on cyber threats to command, control and communications in the transportation industry.

As a result of the recommendations contained in the PCCIP report, Presidential Decision Directive 63 (PDD-63) was signed in May, 1998. The PDD states that, no later than the year 2000, the United States shall have achieved an initial operating capability, to achieve and maintain the ability to protect our critical infrastructure from intentional acts that would significantly diminish the abilities of the Federal government to perform essential national security missions; and the private sector to ensure the orderly functioning of the economy and the delivery of essential transportation services.

Led by the National Security Council (NSC), the Federal government is aggressively working to meet the requirements of PDD-63, identifying vulnerabilities in all of the critical infrastructures, developing action plans to reduce vulnerabilities (focusing primarily on

threats to information systems), and providing outreach and education to the various sectors. The Department of Transportation plays a critical role in these endeavors as the lead for the transportation sector.

Therefore, it was determined that this study would not address information security issues, as it is presumed to be redundant to the work of the PCCIP and NSC and its subcommittees as they continue their efforts to address the requirements of the PDD.

Vulnerability/Impact Assessment Methodology

The methodology employed in this study included the identification of potential threats, the analysis of potential impacts and the identification of potential measures that will mitigate harm to humans and operations. *This analysis does not evaluate the probability of a particular threat occurring (which requires intelligence information).* Therefore, this is not a risk analysis, which would incorporate both the impact of an attack and the probability of the attack being launched. The focus here is on the vulnerabilities of the infrastructure elements to threats and the impact of these attacks.

The analysis methodology includes nine steps:

1. Modal asset identification
2. Key asset selection
3. Threat identification
4. Formulation of scenarios
5. Vulnerability assessment for each scenario
6. Assessment of impacts
7. Assignment of modal vulnerability/impact ratings
8. Assignment of vulnerability/impact ratings across modes
9. Identification of potential countermeasures

These steps (shown in Figure 1) enabled the development of a consistent and logical set of ratings of the vulnerability of transportation assets to typical threats and the impact of a successful attack. It then allowed the development of a list of countermeasures and recommendations to decrease these vulnerabilities.

Specifically, the following was considered for each step:

Step 1 - Modal Asset Identification

Assets were identified by DOT and/or industry professionals based on their expert knowledge of the systems. Facilities, vehicles and equipment (and their functions) of each surface transportation mode and transfer facility were considered.

Step 2 - Key Asset Selection

The assets identified in the previous step were screened in terms of criticality. Criticality is defined as the extent of impact on people, system operations, or both. For example, the loss of a rail control system may profoundly affect the ability of the system to provide service, but may have little impact on humans. The loss of a transit station has a high impact on the passengers who use the system, but may have a less significant impact on the system as a whole, depending on the particular station and rerouting capabilities.

An analytical tool developed by the General Accounting Office (GAO) was used to identify critical transportation assets[2]. This process requires the use of expert opinion to determine how essential the asset is to both the transportation system's ability to provide service, and to the passengers and employees who use and operate the system. Table 1 presents the format of the asset criticality matrix used in this analysis.

Table 1. Asset Criticality Matrix

Transportation System Assets	Asset Loss Impact on	
	People	System
(Asset)	High Medium Low	High Medium Low

---

[2] GAO, *Domestic Terrorism: Prevention Efforts in Selected Federal Courts and Mass Transit Systems,* 1988.

The assets identified in Step 1 above were rated (high, medium or low) for their impact on "people" and the "system." The assets which were rated high in either of these two categories became the targets used in the vulnerability/impact scenarios.

Step 3 - Threat Identification

This step requires the identification of specific threats to critical transportation assets. The threats of interest here are defined as deliberate actions intended to cause injury or death to passengers, employees or the general public, or damage or loss of critical assets.

Threats can identified using both historical (trend) data of all attacks committed against transportation targets, and surveys/interviews of transportation security professionals providing expert opinion.

Step 4 - Formulation of Scenarios

A scenario-based approach can be used to analyze vulnerabilities and impacts. In this step, the critical assets identified in Step 2 and the key threats identified in Step 3 are paired into scenarios to focus the assessments. The emphasis is on generating "illustrative" scenarios which cover a range of potential threats to likely assets. This allows for detailed analysis concerning the likely impacts. Scenarios can be selected in one of two ways:

- Scenarios based on past incident
- Scenarios chosen to represent incidents which have never occurred but are considered reasonably possible.

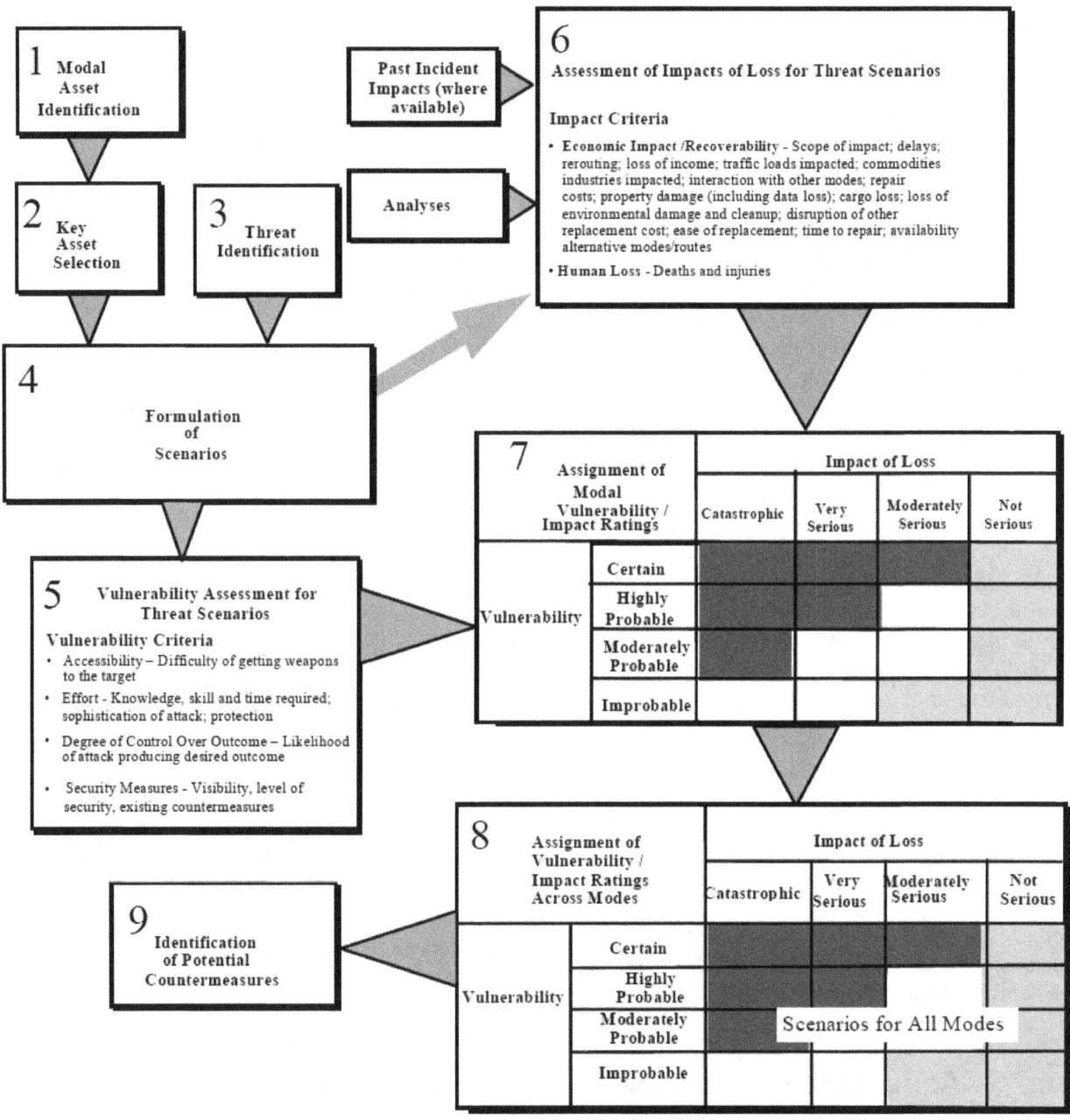

Figure 1. Vulnerability / Impact Process Flow Chart

Step 5 - Vulnerability Assessment for Each Scenario

Once a scenario has been chosen, a determination can be made regarding the vulnerability of the asset to the given attack. Vulnerabilities are physical, technical, administrative, procedural, or human-related characteristics of an asset which make it difficult for a specific attack to be successful. Assignment of these vulnerability ratings was based on the judgment of the investigators. The factors to be considered in the determination of vulnerability includ:

- **Accessibility** - The difficulty of getting the 'weapon' to the target. For example, a highway bridge is easily accessible by a truck bomb. A transit tunnel, however, is much less accessible for placing a charge in the tunnel itself.

- **Effort** - This incorporates two elements - the sophistication of the attack, and the physical resistance of the target. Exploding a device in a truck parked next to a target may require little sophistication, while destroying a bridge with a manageable amount of strategically placed explosive would be more complex.

- **Degree of Control Over Outcome** – The control the perpetrator has over the sequence of events after the attack is initiated. This is a measure of how often this sort of attack would tend to have the desired outcome. For example, detonating an explosive device will virtually always affect the target in a predictable way. However, placing a biological device with a timed trigger may not result in the intended exposure if the wind conditions (and other factors) are unfavorable.

- **Security Measures** – These include such factors as security devices, patrols, and visibility.

Scenarios are then rated for each of these factors and a total vulnerability number determined. The total score is assigned a likelihood of loss category (see Table 2).

Step 6 - Assessment of Impacts

Successful attacks against transportation assets can create an impact in several ways. First, there is the human loss, in terms of fatalities and injuries. Then there are the direct costs of the property which has been destroyed, repair costs and cleanup costs. There are also the costs of the disruptions in service - from the time lost while the system is not functioning or travel and shipments are rerouted, to the costs to businesses

relying on just-in-time production which do not receive their parts in time. Finally, there is the loss of public confidence in the transportation system.

This analysis focused on the losses from property damage, disruption of service and death and injury, rather than on the harder to quantify values such as loss of confidence and impact on manufacturing.

The factors used to assess impact of loss were:

Economic Impact / Recoverability. This focused on the total economic impacts of the successful attack. In arriving at an estimate of the impact, investigators considered the following factors:

- Degree of disruption (e.g., is the system brought to a standstill or can it operate at reduced capacity?)
- Availability of backup systems
- Volume handled by the asset
- Cost of repair/replacement (structures and vehicles)
- Cargo loss and property damage
- Time to repair
- Disruption of commerce
- Costs of delay (include interaction with other modes)
- Delays to general public
- Cost of rerouting/diversions/alternate modes
- Response costs - rescue activities and evacuation of threatened population
- Cleanup costs (debris) for damaged structures and vehicles
- Cleanup costs (hazmat) for hazardous materials removal and decontamination.

Human Loss. Two types of human losses were considered in this study: loss of life and injury.

Table 2. Likelihood of Loss Rating Matrix

Likelihood of Loss Given Attack	Score	
Accessibility		
Easily access ble (ingress and egress); no obstacles; asset is in the open or near the perimeter; asset is reachable without accessing the site (i.e., it can be targeted from a remote site)	5	
Asset is access ble with adequate planning; minimal obstacles to overcome to reach asset; asset in open	4	
Asset is accessible; several obstacles; asset somewhat difficult to reach	3	
Not readily accessible; requires extensive planning and resources to gain access; numerous obstacles to overcome; asset location is difficult to reach	2	
Extremely difficult to access; numerous obstacles	1	
Effort - protection design, sophistication of attack		
Requires little skill, few resources, and minimal time; no precautionary measures exist to prevent intentional damage	5	
Requires limited knowledge, skills, and abilities to neutralize; requires few resources and little time to destroy, damage or steal the asset	4	
Requires some knowledge and training; requires limited resources and time to destroy, damage or steal the asset	3	
Hardened to prevent damage; requires extensive knowledge, skills, and abilities to destroy, damage, or steal the asset	2	
Difficult to damage; hardened site to prevent damage; virtually impenetrable or prone to sabotage	1	
Degree of Control Over Outcome - control perpetrator has over sequence of events after attack is initiated		
Attack directly harms target; attack not susceptible to outside factors	5	
Attack harms target almost directly; minor susceptibility to outside factors	4	
Simple sequence of events involved; some susceptibility to outside factors	3	
Device is complex; attack quite susceptible to outside factors	2	
Success dependent on complex sequence of events following initiation of attack; attack highly susceptible to outside factors (weather conditions, electrical transmissions, dispersal of materials to intended targets)	1	
Security Measures - security devices, patrols, visibility		
No security measures for the asset; not susceptible to outside factors	5	
Minimal security (e.g., fence only); remote site	4	
Limited security measures (i.e., lights, patrols, no electronic measures); located in remote area	3	
Medium level of security (i.e., lights, patrols, early warning and anti-intrusion devices); located in large, built-up area	2	
High security level; 100% active armed security force; asset has electronic surveillance, anti-intrusion, or early warning device; highly visible to public; located in large built-up area	1	
	Total	
Likelihood of Loss Given Attack Rating Certain 17-20 Highly Probable 13-16 Moderately Probable 9-12 Improbable 4-8		

This analysis utilized the Consequence Assessment Tool Set (CATS), a computer-based modeling tool which allows assessment of the consequences of natural and technological (including Weapons of Mass Destruction (WMD)) disasters to population, resources and infrastructure. The CATS Chemical/ Biological/Nuclear (CBN) transport and dispersion models and high explosives (HE) model were used in several of the scenarios to estimate the total number of persons affected, as well as the severity and extent of damage to property and infrastructure.

The CATS was developed under the guidance of the U.S. Defense Special Weapons Agency (DSWA) and the Federal Emergency Management Agency (FEMA). Other users include the Department of Energy (DOE, the Federal Bureau of Investigation (FBI), and the

Table 3. Impact of Loss Rating Matrix

Impact of Loss Given Attack	Score	
Economic Impact/Recoverability - scope of impact; traffic volumes impacted; industries impacted; high operational costs; supported areas impacted; proximity to populated areas; cargo loss; loss of property or data; ease of replacement; time to repair; evacuations		
High traffic volume; rerouting or alternative modes requires much effort; high operational costs; high cleanup/response costs; significant impacts to multiple modes; destruction or damage results in extended operational disruption	10	
Moderate to high traffic volume; some rerouting or alternative modes required; asset can be repaired or replaced, but recovery is difficult	8	
Moderate traffic volume; moderate delays; moderate operational costs; moderate cleanup/response costs; repairs or replacement are moderately difficult	6	
Some delays rerouting not required; repairs are relatively easy	4	
Low traffic volume; low delays; alternative routes readily available; low operational costs; no impact on other areas; repairs are not difficult	2	
No significant economic Impact	0	
Human Loss - Likelihood of human loss		
High Human Loss (50 or more deaths)	10	
Moderate-High Human Loss (20-49 deaths)	8	
Moderate Human Loss (10-19 deaths)	6	
Low-Moderate Human Loss (5-9 deaths)	4	
Low Human Loss (1-4 deaths)	2	
Human loss unlikely (no deaths; few, minor injuries at most)	0	
	Total	

Impact of Loss Rating

Catastrophic	16-20	
Very Serious	11-15	
Moderately Serious	6-10	
Not Serious	2-5	

U.S. Corps of Engineers. This tool will reside in RSPA's Office of Emergency Transportation (OET).

Once scores for human loss and economic cost were assigned, these were then combined into Table 3.

Step 7 - Assignment of Modal Vulnerability/Impact Ratings

Each scenario at this point has been assigned a rating for both vulnerability and impact of loss. The purpose of this step is to combine these scores and present them in a way that provides insight into which scenarios are of the greatest concern.

All of the scenarios from each mode are placed in the matrix (Table 4) based on the ratings assigned in Steps 5 and 6 above. The columns represent the level of impact, decreasing from

left to right. The rows show the vulnerability, with lower entries less vulnerable.

Finally, when all of the scenarios have been placed in the matrix, they are checked to ensure consistency in the ratings for that mode.

Step 8 - Assignment of Vulnerability/Impact Ratings Across Modes

After all of the modal vulnerability/impact grids have been generated, they are combined into a master matrix, containing all scenarios. This matrix is reviewed by a panel comprised of experts representing each of the modes. The panel ensures that the scores are consistent across modes, and the resulting matrix accurately portrayed the relative impacts and vulnerabilities of the scenarios.

This matrix is divided into three priority levels. The category of greatest concern, shown in the top left corner of the matrix, includes scenarios classified as:

- Certain/Catastrophic
- Certain/Very Serious
- Certain/Moderately Serious
- Highly Probably/Catastrophic
- Highly Probable/Very Serious
- Moderately Probable/Catastrophic

The second category of scenarios, in the middle of the matrix, still warrant careful consideration, although the level of concern is less. This includes scenarios rated as:

- Highly Probable / Moderately Serious
- Moderately Probable / Very Serious
- Moderately Probable / Moderately Serious
- Improbable / Catastrophic

- Improbable / Very Serious

The final category, shown in the lower right corner of the matrix, comprises the Not Serious as well as Improbable/Moderately Serious scenarios of lower priority.

Step 9 - Identification of Potential Countermeasures

This step involves the identification of proposed countermeasures to address vulnerabilities. Countermeasures may include physical modification, police and security deployment and staffing alternatives, security technology, environmental design and review, security materials selection and analysis, administrative and operational, procedural changes, education/training, or other measures that will reduce the vulnerability and/or impact.

Table 4. Vulnerability/Impacts Matrix

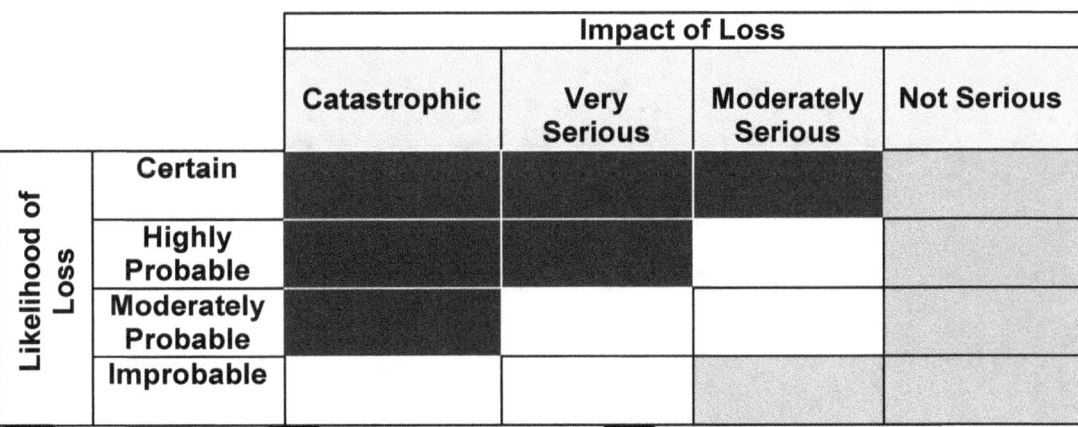

MEANS OF THREAT DELIVERY 2

This section describes a range of means by which to deliver a credible threat to the Nation's transportation infrastructure. The sources of such threats can be broadly categorized as *domestic* and *international* terrorism. *Domestic terrorism* occurs in the United States and is perpetrated by U.S.-based groups. *International* terrorism can occur in the U.S. or against U.S. citizens and property in other nations, and is perpetrated by foreign-based groups or directed by countries or groups outside the U.S. whose activities transcend national boundaries. International terrorism can be state-sponsored or committed by non-state actors.

Threats to transportation infrastructure can be grouped into two categories. The first are considered physical threats, which require relatively direct contact with the target to inflict damage or disruption of service. Possible sources of physical threats include explosives, chemical and biological weapons, the redirection of hazardous materials (including nuclear materials), as well as direct physical manipulation of personnel. The second category of threats is referred to as informational (or cyber) threats because they inflict damage through destruction or disruption of information used to control the physical assets. This may involve causing damage to the control devices through direct attack, as in the case of electromagnetic weapons (High Energy Radio Frequency "HERF" guns, Electromagnetic Pulse Transformer Bombs) or less direct but no less disruptive computer viruses. An examination of these threats follows.

Potential Surface Transportation Targets

Scenarios developed to assess vulnerabilities rely on the pairing of threats to critical assets. (The relative criticality of the asset is determined by a qualitative assessment of the impact on people or the overall system if the asset were attacked.) While varying across modes under study, all identified critical assets fall into the following five categories:

- Facilities (e.g., stations, terminals, ports, fuel transfer centers)

- Means of conveyance (e.g., roads, tunnels and bridges, tracks, waterways, pipelines)

- Vehicles (e.g., trains, trucks, ships, buses)

- Supporting structures (e.g., power substations, locks and dams,)

- Control/Information technology (e.g., signal systems, Supervisory Control And Data Acquisition System (SCADA), navigational aids/GPS, cargo tracking systems, EDI)

Categories of Means of Attack – Definitions and Historical Background

Explosives, cyber attacks, weapons of mass destruction (WMD), sabotage, and armed assault/hostage/barricade situations are categories of threats to which transportation systems are subject.

Explosives. Historically, explosives have been the most common means utilized by terrorists or those wishing to perpetrate extreme acts of violence. For purposes of this assessment, threats from explosives are categorized into two classifications. The first classification includes those threats to the transportation infrastructure arising from the use of a small quantity of explosives. Examples of this type of threat include the 1995 and 1997 bombings of the Paris Metro, bus bombings in Israel, and the 1996 bombing of India's national railroad. The second classification includes threats resulting from the use of a larger quantity of explosives. Examples include the World Trade Center bombing, the Oklahoma City bombing, and the bombing of U.S. military housing in Saudi Arabia.

Cyber Attacks. This relatively new means of attack involves the intentional manipulation of computer hardware or software to disable information systems, to deny service from these systems, or to destroy or manipulate data stored within these systems. Examples of this threat include viruses, unauthorized access to computer networks, and intentional misuse of information systems.

Weapons of Mass Destruction (WMD). This category of threat includes the use of chemical, biological, or nuclear weapons, agents, or contaminants (nuclear weapons are not considered herein). While there has been limited historical evidence documenting the use of such weapons, many of which are banned through worldwide treaties, recent seizures and monitoring of terrorist activity indicate the viability of this threat. The sarin attack committed against the Tokyo subway system in 1995 marked the first time a terrorist group has successfully deployed this type of weapon against a civilian population.

Sabotage. This category of threat may or may not involve tools and tactics traditionally

classified as terrorist. Due to the potential for disruption, destruction, and casualties, however, sabotage is included in this assessment. An example of this type of threat is the derailment of Amtrak's *Sunset Limited* in Arizona.

Armed Assaults, Hostage, and Barricade Situations. This type of threat includes traditional terrorist activity such as the 1985 hijacking of the *Achille Lauro* and those acts of extreme violence that are not classified as terrorism but have extreme consequences for the transportation industry, such as the 1993 Long Island Railroad shooting.

Physical Threats - Characteristics

Since threats of a physical nature have most frequently been associated with bombings, the first description will be of explosives characteristics and availability. This is followed by a description of some issues surrounding hazardous materials. The section then describes briefly some aspects of chemical and biological threats, before concluding the description of physical threats with a mention of the direct manipulation of personnel.

Explosives

Many high explosives are relatively easy to manufacture. For example, ANFO, used in the Oklahoma City bombing og 1995, can readily be formulated from ammonium nitrate and fuel oil. A partial listing of explosive formulations found in the do-it-yourself terrorist literature is given in Table 7.

In addition to manufacturing explosives, theft is a direct means of acquisition. The Bureau of Alcohol, Tobacco and Firearms (BATF) reports that many different types of explosives are reported stolen in the U.S., so access to such weapons through theft is probable (see Table 8).

Table 5.   Other High Explosives[3]

Explosive Name	Characteristics
RDX	150% more powerful than TNT and easier to detonate (also called cyclonite).
ANFO (Ammonium nitrate fuel oil solution)	Same characteristics as ammonium nitrate except the fuel oil prevents the ammonium nitrate from absorbing moisture from the air which inhibits detonation in some cases. ANFO requires a large shockwave to set it off. A triggering explosion initiates an exothermic chemical reaction between the nitrogen compounds and hydrocarbons in the fuel oil.
POTASSIUM CHLORATE	Combined with petroleum jelly is slightly more powerful than black powder. It must be confined while passing a shockwave through it to detonate.
NITROSTARCH EXPLOSIVES	Various starches treated with a mixture of concentrated nitric and sulfuric acids. These explosives are slightly less powerful than TNT but not as difficult to detonate.
PICRIC ACID (Tri-Nitro-Phenol)	Typically used as booster charge in conjunction with other explosives. It is fairly easy to make with concentrated sulfuric and nitric acids. It has a tendency to form unstable salts when placed in metal containers.
AMMONIUM PICRATE (Explosive-D)	Made from picric acid and household ammonia. Requires a substantial shock wave to detonate.
LEAD AZIDE	Combination of sodium azide and lead acetate. It is usually used as a booster charge and can be detonated using heat from igniter wire or blasting caps.
DYNAMITE	Made by adding inert material to nitroglycerine. A commercial product used for a variety of construction and mining related activities. Requires blasting caps for detonation.

Table 6. Explosives Stolen During 1990-1994

Item Stolen	Quantity Reported Stolen
Dynamite	35,334 lbs.
Blasting Agents	25,461 lbs.
Boosters	4,042 lbs.
Primers	677 lbs.
Black Powder	586 lbs.
Grenades	312 units
TNT, C4	184 lbs.
Smokeless Powder	74 lbs.

An explosive is a   substance which reacts chemically to produce heat and gas with rapid expansion of matter. A detonation is a very special type of explosion. It is a rapid chemical reaction, initiated by the heat accompanying a shock compression, which liberates sufficient energy, before any expansion occurs, to sustain the shock wave. A shock wave propagates into the unreacted material at supersonic speed (1,500-9,000 m/s). Explosives are generally categorized as high or low explosives. Low explosives, also called propellants, undergo fast burn, rather than detonation. High explosives, with proper initiation, can detonate.

Among high explosives are those that have penetrating power, commercial explosives. Two high explosives common in military use are TNT (2,4,6-trinitrotoluene) and RDX (cyclotrimethylenetrinitramine). These explosives are quite different chemically. Thus, they differ in physical characteristics and performance properties. TNT can be melted and cast into a desired shape. RDX must be mixed with other materials to make it shapable. The

---

[3] The Terrorist's Handbook, Section 3.3, http://phoenix.phreebyrd.com.

U.S. military uses a formulation of RDX called C4; it is 91% RDX and 9% plasticizer (mainly bis(-2-ethylhexyl) adipate)). Most commercial explosives are formulations of ammonium nitrate with fuel – the most common of which is ANFO.

Because TNT has been used extensively, its performance is often the benchmark against wich other explosives are measured. Explosive scientists usually characterize the power of an explosive by its detonation velocity. However, from the prospective of structural damage, explosive performance is equated to blast overpressure or impulse (See Table 7). Explosives are formed of four types of atoms: carbon (C), hydrogen (H), oxygen (O), and nitrogen (N). Upon detonation, exothermic (heat releasing) reactions transform nitrogen atoms to form gaseous products (H_2O, CO, or CO_2). The produced heat and gas produce an air blast, which causes most of the structural damage.

Table 7. Relative Destructive Force of Explosives

Explosive Type	Detonation Velocity (km/s)	Overpressure Conversion Factor	Charge Required
TNT	6.94	1	1 lb.
RDX	8.64	1.3	0.75 lbs.
ANFO	5	0.4	2.4 lbs.

The magnitude of the blast depends on the nature of the explosive and is proportional to its size (weight, W) and inversely proportional to the distance from the explosive. The air blast travels radially outward from the ignition source of the detonation. Thus, an explosive material placed at close proximity to a structure will have maximum destructive effect, while explosive placed some distance from the targeted area will have significantly less impact. The magnitude of the shock wave decays exponentially as it travels away from the source, and that decay is related to the cube of the distance (R) from the source. Unless the explosive charge was suspended in air, the blast wave from its detonation is quickly reflected off the ground. When the blast wave encounters the ground or any other solid structure, it is reflected. The reflected wave interacts with the still oncoming wave. Depending on the location of the interaction, the interference can be positive, resulting in amplification of the shock wave, or negative, resulting in a lessening of the shock.

$$\text{Explosion Pressure} \propto W/R^3$$

This equation shows how blast overpressure varies with explosive weight and distance. The equation implies that doubling the standoff distance reduces the incident pressure by a factor of eight. Therefore, the single most effective way to minimize damage to a structure is to increase the distance between the target and the source of the explosion.

The equation above and most blast analysis codes require the input of the TNT "equivalent" weight of an explosive. The equivalence is not exact. Equivalence can be measured as the peak overpressure or the impulse of a detonation. For example, to determine the TNT equivalence of 1 lb. of ANFO, the calculation is straightforward:

TNT equivalence of ANFO = (Pressure from 1 lb. ANFO) / (Pressure from 1 lb. TNT).

The problem is where to measure the overpressure. The ANFO/TNT ratio will vary depending on the distance the pressure transducer is (10 ft. or 20 ft.) from the explosive. One reason for this is the positive and negative interference factors discussed above. The TNT equivalence will be yet another value if impulse (defined as the area under the peak vs. time curve) is used instead of overpressure. Therefore, TNT equivalencies should not be considered to have a high degree of precision nor accuracy. Nevertheless they are used in many blast damage calculations.

Often the most common evidence of an explosive blast is the presence of a crater. Figure 2 shows a diagram of a crater produced by 100 pounds of C4 detonated at ground level in dry sandy soil. The crater is over three feet deep and almost eleven feet across. By comparison, the ANFO device used in Oklahoma City at the Alfred Murrah Federal

Building bombing resulted an eight foot deep, 30-foot wide crater. Roughly 6,000 cubic feet of soil was blown away. Although cratering is dependent on the type and degree of compaction of the soil, it is safe to assume the ANFO charge was much larger than the TNT equivalence of the 100 pounds of C4. Given some knowledge of a structure's material, dimensions and construction technique, it is possible to determine the type and quantity of explosive needed to destroy a structure.

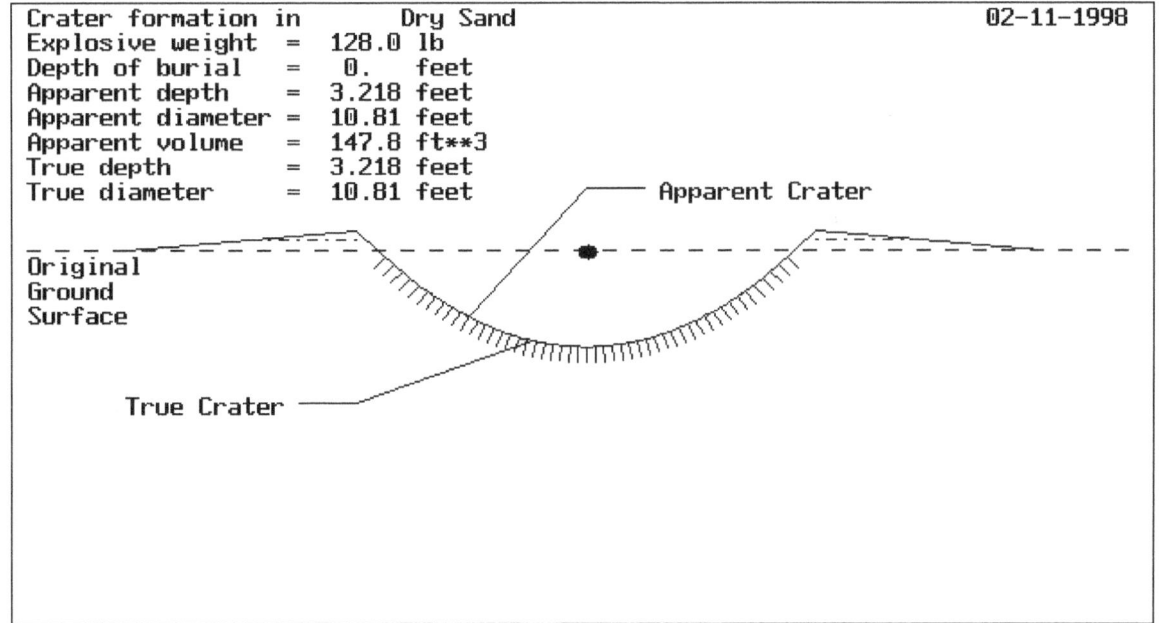

Figure 2. Crater Resulting From Detonation of 100 Pounds of C4 at Ground Level

Armor-piercing Weapons

Armor-piercing weapons with high energy explosives are designed to hit and penetrate heavily protected objects, often while they are moving. These weapons have warheads that are capable of penetrating thick steel or masonry and then destroy the object from within. Many types of armor-piercing weapons have been produced for anti-tank applications and these are thought to be widely available, either by theft or black market purchase. First generation shoulder-fired anti-tank weapons first appeared during World War II and continued through the 1950s. Second generation devices evolved during the 1960s that were able to penetrate roughly a foot of armor. More recent devices

produced since the mid 1980s can penetrate up to three feet of armor. This last class of devices represent third generation weapons (see Table 8).

Hazardous Materials

Many substances are classified as hazardous material (hazmat). These materials include fuels (gasoline, diesel, aviation), liquefied petroleum gases, most lubricants, solvents, organic and inorganic manufacturing chemicals. The primary danger that these substances pose to infrastructure are incidents that occur during transportation. These types of incidents have occurred due to random accidents on all of the Nation's transportation systems. Policy and guidelines established by regulatory agencies concerning movement of hazmat have minimized this class of problem. More compelling concerns are explosions and spills of hazardous materials that are precipitated or stimulated by terrorist activity. These events manifest the same impact as explosives, described above, or chemical weapons, which are described in the following section.

In 1977 there were over 1.1 billion tons of hazardous chemical and petroleum products transported over our nation's highways.[4] This number has steadily increased over the past twenty years to a total of 4 billion tons shipped annually.[5] The tonnage mix between chemical and petroleum products is roughly equal. However, chemical shipments represent about two thirds of the total miles of hazardous material transported. In addition, pipelines transported 5.5 billion barrels of petroleum in 1996. The U.S. Pipeline network transports about 60% of the crude oil and petroleum products that fuel the Nation's industries and economy, as well as individual households.

Hazardous material used as weapons could rely upon conventional explosives to precipitate an accident involving hazmat. Examples might include a deliberate attack on a propane truck or rail car, or setting out to release radioactive material in the form of spent fuel. This latter approach would both physically destroy a target and contaminate the surrounding area. Decontamination would be costly and the effects long lasting, since radioactive materials cannot be decontaminated in the same way as chemical or biological agents. Radioactive material must be removed and contained to allow the material to decay naturally. Radioactive residue can, however, generally be detected far easier than chemical or biological contaminants.

---

[4] Domenic Maio, Tai-Kuo Liu, "Truck Transportation of Hazardous Material, A National Overview," DOT-TSC-RSPA-87-8, December 1987.

[5] NTSB Testimony before the Committee on Appropriations Subcommittee on Transportation and Related Agencies, House of Representatives, March 7, 1996, http://www.ntsb.gov/speeches/JH960307.

Table 8. Variety of Anti-Tank Weapons[6]

Weapon Name	Source Country	Weight	Range	Warhead Dia./Wt.	Armor Penetration
Milan Anti-Tank Missile	France	32 kg	2000 m	133 mm/3.12 kg	>1000 mm
Eryx Anti-Tank Missile	France	21 kg	600 m	160 mm/ 3.8 kg	900 mm
Panzerfaust 3 Anti-Tank Launcher	Germany	13 kg	300 m	110 mm/NA	>700 mm
Folgore Anti-Tank System	Italy	21 kg	4500 m	80 mm/3 kg	>450 mm
Apilas	South Africa	9 kg	330 m	112 mm/NA	>720 mm
RPG-7 Anti-Tank Launcher	Soviet Union	11 kg	300 m	85 mm/NA	330 mm
C-90-C Weapon System	Spain	5 kg	200 m	90 mm/NA	500 mm
AT-4 Anti-Tank Launcher	Sweden	7 kg	300 m	84 mm/NA	>400 mm
Carl Gustav M2 Recoilless Gun	Sweden	15 kg	700 m	84 mm/NA	>400 mm
LAW 80 Anti-tank Launcher	U.K.	9 kg	500 m	94 mm/NA	700 mm
M72 66mm Anti-tank Launcher	USA	4 kg	220 m	66 mm/NA	350 mm
SMAW	USA	14 kg	500 m	83 mm/NA	>600 mm
AT-8 Bunker Buster	USA	8 kg	250 m	84 mm/NA	NA
Superdragon Anti-tank Missile	USA	17 kg	1500 m	140 mm/10.07 kg	>500 mm
TOW 2 Anti-tank Missile	USA	116 kg	3750 m	127 mm/28 kg	>700 mm
Javelin AAWS/M	USA	16 kg	2000 m	127 mm/NA	>400 mm

Chemical and Biological Weapons

Chemical weapons are designed to cause injury or death in humans, rather than property, and can exist in a solid, liquid or gaseous state. They can be dispersed using a variety of delivery systems, the simplest of which include breakable containers or aerosols. Typically, the means of exposure to a chemical is passive through inhalation or direct absorption through skin, eyes and mucous membranes. An inhaled agent will damage the lungs and then pass rapidly into the bloodstream. Other exposure methods can involve oral ingestion of an agent that will damage the digestive system and then move into the bloodstream. Rapid acting chemical agents can cause symptoms to appear almost immediately while slower acting agents may take days before the first symptoms appear.

Chemical weapons can be classified principally as Choking agents, Blood agents, Blister agents, Nerve agents and Tear agents. There are relatively few chemical and biological agents capable of being fielded in large-scale situations.

While it is likely that hundreds or perhaps thousands of possible agents have been studied by the U.S. military, seven have had all the properties required, including potency and stability, to use in munitions.

Biological weapons, like chemical weapons, will not directly impact the transportation infrastructure but, instead, cause injury to users. Biological weapons (BW) rely upon pathogens (bacteria, viruses and fungi) or toxins as the active agent to achieve debilitating physiological effects upon targeted populations. Pathogens are self-replicating organisms that cause serious disease in humans or animals. Several well known deadly pathogens include organisms that cause anthrax, botulism, tularemia, plague and Q-fever. Organisms can also be grown in a laboratory to produce toxins, which are metabolism by-products of the organism that are poisonous to humans. Toxins are usually proteins or peptides that act upon specific receptors in the body and alter normal physiological functions of the body. Most toxins are relatively unstable and must be stored

---

[6] Hogg, I.V., "Infantry Support Weapons: Mortars, Missiles, and Machine Guns," Greenhill Military Manual No. 5, London: Greenhill Books, Lionel Leventhal Limited, 1995.

within controlled environmental conditions, since heat and other traumatic factors effect them.[7] Biological agents are often undetectable by human senses. Furthermore, there are no widely available biological detection devices used by state or local governments that can reliably inform of the presence of these biological pathogens.

There are roughly fifty credible biological agents that have been investigated for use in biological warfare. Examination of desirable characteristics of these agents, and ranking them from the prospective of a potential terrorist, results in twenty-two likely candidates among those fifty biological agents (see Table 9).[8] These agents are easy to produce, store well and can be disbursed using aerosol techniques.

Biological weapons were tested by the U.S. military during the Cold War to assess vulnerability to attack. Simulated releases were carried out in several subway systems, with detection equipment set up to measure dispersion rates and toxicity.[9] More recently, the first operational military unit established specifically to deal with the aftermath of a terrorist assault employing a weapon of mass destruction has been established.[10]

Direct Manipulation of Personnel

The last in the discussion of physical threats is the direct interference with or manipulation of personnel, either drivers of vehicles or operators of some part of the transportation infrastructure. This may include hostage taking, hijacking, and armed assaults.

Information Threats

Terrorist attacks have typically targeted single assets such as individuals or buildings. More sophisticated informational attacks in the future may exploit emerging vulnerabilities associated with the complexity and interconnection of new infrastructure technologies. Intelligent Transportation Systems (ITS) utilize new information infrastructures to improve capacity or provide better service without extending the physical assets, and will be discussed in a later section.

Attacks on information systems may be motivated by the thrill, financial gain, or notoriety they symbolize. Whatever the motivation, success in altering data, extracting information, or introducing viruses can do serious damage to U.S. infrastructure assets.

Information Warfare (IWAR) Weapons

Software applications are increasingly embedded into critical information systems. Failure of such systems have the potential to cause catastrophic impact and loss of life. These types of weapons are difficult to detect and countermeasures can prove to be very expensive. With electromagnetic weapons, terrorists can achieve low-risk high-visibility attacks upon critical information systems. Terrorists will be able to fashion such devices as they become more technologically capable in tactics and strategies in the coming decades.[11]

---

[7] "The Biological & Chemical Warfare Threat," anon.

[8] Greenwood, "A Relative Assessment of Putative Biological-Warfare Agents," MIT Lincoln Labs, July 17, 1997.

[9] Mayer, Terry, USAF, "The Biological Weapon: A Poor Nation's Weapon of Mass Destruction," http://www.cdsar.af mil/battle/chp8 html

[10] The Chemical-Biological Incident Response Force (CBIRF), as described in Chris Semple, "Consequence Management: Domestic Response to Weapons of Mass Destruction," Parameters, US Army War College Quarterly, Autumn, 1997, and http://carlisle-www.army.mil/usawc/Parameters/97autumn.

[11] Matthew Devost, Brian Houghton and Neal Pollard, "Information Terrorism: Can You Trust Your Toaster?," SAIC, http://www.terrorism.com/terrorism/itpaper.

Table 9. Biological Agents

BACTERIA (9)	VIRUSES (7)	TOXINS (6)
• Anthrax • Q-Fever • Tularemia • Psittacosis • Glanders • RMSF • Melioidosis • Brucellosis • Plague	• Dengue fever • Equine Encephalitis • Hantaan • Congo-Crimean HF • Chikungunya • Variola • Ebola	• Botulinum • SEB • Perfringens • Ricin • Saxitoxin • Tetrodotoxin

Table 10. IWAR Weapons

Attack objective	Weapon
a) Destroy or disrupt information system	• High Energy Radio Frequency (HERF) guns • Electromagnetic Pulse Transformer Bombs (EMP/T)
b) Alter data to force abnormal operation	• Virus • Worm • Trojan Horse

There are two general methods that a terrorist may employ for an information system attack. The first targets an information system itself with the intention of destroying the system or targeting the activities dependent on the information infrastructure. The second method exploits the information system to alter its data in an attempt to force the system to perform abnormal operations (see Table 10).

Software inserted into an information system to cause disruption or damage may also originate from Viruses, Worms and Trojan Horses. These programs infect a system and their impact can vary from inconvenience to total loss of data and failure. Lists of viruses, from the benign to the malicious, can be found in any anti-virus software package for the personal computer.

The trend towards improved computerized control over transportation infrastructure brings with it increased vulnerability to these associated threats.

Electronic weapons are designed to attack computer-based systems. These devices include electromagnetic pulse and radio frequency weapons that are intended to destabilize or destroy sensitive electronic components. Attacks using these weapons typically target key links or nodes whose destruction and failure could ripple through the target infrastructure.

High Energy Radio Frequency (HERF) guns create an impulse of high-energy electromagnetic radiation at radio frequencies that is directly aimed at a target. If the target is not adequately protected from external electromagnetic emissions it will not withstand the induced electromagnetic fields and will quickly fail. Electromagnetic Pulse Transformer Bombs (EMP/T), on the other hand, are similar to HERF devices, but their intensity is on the order of a thousand times greater. Though usually very short in duration, their effect is permanent, since electronic components are overwhelmed and destroyed by intense electromagnetic radiation, rendering them useless for normal system operation.

COUNTERMEASURES 3

This assessment provides the framework, tools, and methodology to assist in making informed decisions to reduce identified surface transportation vulnerabilities.

Summary

To date, the vast majority of resources and activity related to transportation security in the United States has been focused on aviation. As the previous chapters have described, the country's surface transportation systems are also vulnerable to several types of terrorist and criminal attack. A variety of countermeasures must be incorporated into the surface transportation systems to mitigate these vulnerabilities.

A national commitment must be made to surface transportation security. The President's Commission on Critical Infrastructure Protection (PCCIP) has clearly stated in its recent report[12] that the security of the transportation system of the United States is now a national responsibility. Terrorism is directed at the nation as a whole, and not at individual transportation operations. Therefore, an enhanced federal role is appropriate to help reduce the level of vulnerability identified in this report. At the same time, it must be acknowledged that it will not be possible to eliminate completely all vulnerabilities inherent in such a large-scale and public service as transportation.

Among the specific areas where increased federal participation can help are the following:

- Improved communications with others

---

[12]   *Critical Foundations: Protecting America's Infrastructures.* The report of the President's Commission on Critical Infrastructure Protection, October 1997, passim.

involved in transportation security.

- Creating partnerships and consortia involving public and private sectors and the academic and research communities to improve transportation security.

- Facilitating cross-jurisdictional (domestic and international) contacts, information sharing and negotiations on the subject with other organizations and agencies.

- Gathering and analyzing intelligence and information related to potential threats, and disseminating warnings to the appropriate recipients.

- Serving as a central repository and disseminator of information and data related to transportation security, including training, education and awareness materials.

- Providing information on the latest and most effective countermeasures and state-of-the-art "best practices."

- Facilitating research and development into potential new or improved countermeasures with an across-the-board applicability.

The appropriate roles and responsibilities of the various public and private sector organizations and agencies for transportation security should be further clarified, based on an expansion of federal participation. A follow-on effort should be initiated to explore in greater detail the best specific means by which cooperation and collaboration among these agencies can be enhanced. This effort should include representatives from all of the important transportation modes and industries, public sector service providers, the law enforcement and intelligence communities, the American business community, and the general public.

One of the tasks will be to identify necessary changes to legislation and administrative procedures.

System operators must be accountable for implementing effective countermeasure solutions. It remains the case that the primary responsibility for assuring the safety and security of those using a transportation service resides with the provider of that service. As the White House Commission on Aviation Safety and Security recommended for airports, managers of other transportation systems should work with their stakeholders to assess their systems' vulnerabilities and develop and implement security strategies accordingly. However, the recent and worrisome increase in terrorism directed against transportation requires a modified approach.

Circumstances warranting direct federal role. The Federal government has a direct responsibility in specific cases where national security could be negatively affected by a successful terrorist assault on a transportation target. Such situations include: enhancing the security of key links between a military base and a seaport or airport necessary to deploy military assets during a crisis; or providing for redundancy and backup capabilities for key public assets – such as air traffic control, maritime navigation or metropolitan Intelligent Transportation Infrastructure installations – whose degradation could have significant negative consequences.

Countermeasures must be coordinated through partnerships. The PCCIP identified many ways government agencies and the private sector could work together to develop and implement security solutions. The DOT must be an active participant in collaborative activities for R&D into broadly applicable security countermeasures and deployment of the results to ensure positive impacts throughout the national transportation system. DOT can also encourage the creation of research consortia under existing federal technology transfer mechanisms such as Cooperative Research and Development Agreements (CRADAs). If necessary, exemptions from competitive practices legislation could also be sought.

Efforts and resources must be focused on actual threats. This report identifies many serious vulnerabilities in the nation's surface transportation system. Most of these vulnerabilities are found in the physical infrastructure and daily operations, since damage to those aspects of the transportation system carries the potential for the most serious consequences. In the near future, however, serious vulnerabilities will increasingly be found within the information and communications infrastructures that are rapidly evolving in parallel to the existing physical transportation network. As these systems themselves become more complex and interdependent, they also become more vulnerable to possible disruptions. The negative consequences of such disruptions also escalate as the transportation system becomes increasingly dependent on these support infrastructures. Disruptions can arise from many sources: blunders and unintentional errors, natural disasters, outside hackers, disgruntled insiders, criminals, industrial sabotage, terrorism, intelligence gathering, or even deliberate information warfare. A more comprehensive depiction of the current and near-term vulnerabilities of the national transportation system, including both physical and 'cyber' dimensions, can best be obtained by considering this surface transportation vulnerability assessment in conjunction with other recent studies of this subject, particularly those by the PCCIP and White House Commission on Aviation Safety and Security.

In acting upon these recommendations and conclusions, however, the latest and most credible intelligence data and analyses must be consulted. This will help to assure that investments in countermeasures can be focused where the threat levels and the potential level of consequences are the highest. The DOT should work closely with the intelligence and law enforcement communities to develop the most accurate picture of current and future threats which could exploit transportation system vulnerabilities. It should also work with public and private transportation system operators to ensure that countermeasures are directed at these areas.

Key near-term improvements should be implemented immediately. Many existing countermeasures can be readily implemented to reduce vulnerabilities in the near-term.

- The physical security of transportation facilities can be improved through installing existing technologies and systems for such purposes as perimeter and access controls, monitoring, surveillance, and intrusion detection.

- The concept of *employee and patron vigilance* is essential to surface transportation security. Measures that support the security awareness, education and training of employees and patrons are critical, particularly in high volume passenger environments and remote facilities.

- A systems approach to security should be employed to ensure maximum effectiveness and compatibility with operational demands and institutional requirements.

Countermeasures for chemical and biological attacks must be developed and implemented. Because of the large numbers of people who could be affected by chemical and biological attacks against surface transportation systems, this topic should receive special emphasis. DOT must work actively with other federal, state and local agencies addressing the possible use of weapons of mass destruction, and effective responses to such an event.

- Models of the behavior of chemical/biological agents in transportation environments, such as subways, must be validated and enhanced.

- Decision support tools must be developed to help transportation operators and first responders take effective action.

- Sensors must be developed and evaluated for use in transportation environments.

- Protection and decontamination equipment must be acquired and made available to meet the needs of high volume passenger transportation systems.

- Extensive training on the nature of the threat, countermeasures and response strategies must be provided to employees at all levels.

- Response plans must be exercised regularly.

Information technology designs must ensure security. Even though the most significant vulnerabilities identified in this report tended to be in the area of physical infrastructure and daily operations, the transportation system is becoming increasingly dependent on information technology. As was specifically pointed out by the PCCIP, transportation applications for monitoring, control, dispatching, management and communications must be protected against information security threats. DOT should work closely with technology providers, transportation operators and other agencies to develop and implement effective information security strategies.

- System architectures and design for large-scale integrated applications such as ITS, as well as individual systems, must include a viable security dimension.

- Security policies and procedures must be developed to ensure compliance throughout the life of the system.

- Extensive awareness building, education and training is needed for all levels of transportation employees.

Information on security incidents, threats and countermeasures must be collected, evaluated and disseminated. Surface transportation security strategies must be based on accurate information on threats and countermeasures.

- Comprehensive data on transportation security incidents must be collected for all modes, and disseminated throughout the transportation and law enforcement communities.

- Timely threat information related to critical transportation system vulnerabilities, as well as effective systems to disseminate this information nationally, must be developed.

- Analysis, modeling and simulations of transportation vulnerabilities and security countermeasures should be developed and exercised, so that countermeasures investments can be more effectively determined.

- DOT should work with other public agencies and the transportation industry to assimilate information on best practices, lessons learned from real life incidents, and the most effective countermeasures systems and procedures.

Recommendations

This section assimilates the recommendations for countermeasures made for each of the modes of transportation, as discussed in Chapter Four. These recommendations have been chosen because of their potential to reduce the vulnerabilities identified in this study, or to mitigate the potential impact on people or the transportation system if these vulnerabilities were exploited. The recommendations address the scenarios evaluated in this report related to terrorism and extreme violence.

Recommendations have been chosen because of their potential to reduce the vulnerabilities identified in this study, or to mitigate the potential impact on people or the transportation system if these vulnerabilities were exploited.

Recommendations have been formulated to address all phases of the countermeasure development life cycle, from assessment of the problem to development and implementation of solutions. They include initiatives which should be addressed by government agencies at the federal, state and local levels; initiatives which should be undertaken by commercial industry; and several initiatives which would be most effectively addressed by public/private partnerships.

Countermeasures, as presented in this report, are strategies, actions, technologies, systems or procedures that can be enacted to reduce a type of vulnerability or the impact of an attack. In relating these recommendations to each of the specific security concerns identified in earlier sections, the reader should be aware that in some cases several countermeasures are needed to mitigate a single vulnerability. In all cases, a comprehensive *systems approach* is needed to formulate the most appropriate set of countermeasures, and to develop the most cost-effective implementation strategy.

These recommendations have been developed as a result of discussions with the DOT Security Working Group, the OST Office of Intelligence and Security, RSPA, various other government agencies, industry groups and researchers, and by the Volpe Center research team conducting this study. They also reflect a close review of other recent studies on this subject, such as the PCCIP and the White House Commission on Aviation Safety and Security.

This is a preliminary set of recommendations, and does not represent all of the initiatives necessary to ensure security of the national surface transportation system. Over the coming year, studies by the National Academy of Sciences and the National Science and Technology Council will further define these recommendations for transportation security countermeasures, and will suggest programmatic approaches and funding requirements to support them.

This section groups countermeasures into three stages:

- Assessing Vulnerabilities
- Developing Solutions
- Implementing Solutions

Stage 1: Assessing Vulnerabilities

In order to define and implement appropriate countermeasures that will address critical security priorities in the nation's transportation infrastructure, the nature of the specific problems in this infrastructure must first be investigated, measured, and analyzed. While this study has identified many categories of vulnerabilities in the nation's transportation system, strategies for reducing these vulnerabilities should be based on comprehensive assessments of specific transportation processes. These assessments must be site-specific studies of the actual transportation facilities and operations, which was beyond the scope of this study.

In addition, the nature of threats to these particular systems and locations is dynamic and must be continually monitored and re-evaluated. Resources for countermeasures will always be scarce, and should be prioritized and focused on actual threats so as to have maximum impact.

This category of recommendations involves data collection and analysis activities necessary to design a focused set of solutions that will address the most pressing current and anticipated concerns:

- *Threat/incident data collection & dissemination* - These activities are needed to clarify the nature and extent of the problems facing the U.S. transportation system, and to make transportation system operators aware of the problems in a timely manner.

- *Risk assessments* - These studies are recommended to generate vulnerability analyses and countermeasure strategies for specific facilities and processes based on actual threat information.

Threat/Incident Data Collection & Dissemination

Develop standards for crime data, data collection technology, regional databases. In many municipalities, incident-based crime reporting has resulted in cost-effective reductions in crime. Local law enforcement agencies have made impressive gains in efficiency by updating both their crime report forms and their crime data management information systems (MIS). Work is needed to provide national standards for transportation police departments concerning crime data and MIS/Record Management Systems (RMS).

Choices made regarding data content, collection, storage, and format dictate the utility of the crime analysis effort. The types of data stored within transportation police/security information systems determine to some degree which issues capture the attention of the transportation system. The arrangement of data within files largely determines the types of analysis that can be performed and the utility of the data for deployment decision-making, case clearance, and the design and evaluation of effective countermeasures. The content and form of information released to the public helps to determine the framework within which the department is held accountable to the community, and plays a significant role in determining public expectations.

Improved information and data on security incidents would assist in development of countermeasures and provide better information for risk management decisions. Some modes of transportation are required to report all safety-related incidents and accidents above a certain threshold, while others report through insurance agreements. These data have been used to establish programs that can prevent and mitigate incidents and lead to cost effective improvements in safety. In some modes, such as public transit, security data is now also being collected. In other modes collection of security data is not required by federal regulation, and is only partially collected by private sector organizations.

The private sector, however, is sometimes reluctant to report security problems, including both physical and cyber attacks, fearing public disclosure of vulnerabilities that could be exploited by others and have a negative impact on public confidence in the industry. Confidential, Freedom of Information Act (FOIA) exempt means of reporting and sharing such information need to be developed.

Develop improved threat data and "warning" system. Modal operations personnel and security forces currently have limited access to the type of intelligence necessary to direct effective terrorism deterrence programs. Enhanced coordination between the private transportation sector and government agencies is essential in improving access to preventative intelligence. A threat database is recommended in order to catalogue incidents such as bomb threats, terrorism, and sabotage that occur throughout the national transportation system. Such a database will provide for enhanced analysis capabilities and will enable the transportation community to better posture itself to manage new and existing threats.

DOT efforts to disseminate threat and other information should be strengthened. A formalized process such as a threat warning system should be established to disseminate designated threat levels and recommend additional activities to be performed to improve deterrence capabilities.

Risk Assessments

As discussed earlier, both site-specific and process-specific risk assessments must be conducted to focus countermeasures and develop effective security strategies. The

assessments must address both physical and information infrastructures. These risk assessments must be based on current and accurate threat information for the location and system being evaluated.

Stage 2: Developing Solutions

This vulnerability assessment has identified many security concerns in need of countermeasures. This section recommends a number of initiatives which are needed to ensure the continued development of new and improved solutions to address these vulnerabilities:

- *Research and development* – Several areas have been identified where initiatives are needed to ensure the development of technologies, systems and procedures that would improve the security of the transportation environment.

- *Standards and guidelines* – Many in the transportation security community feel that guidelines or some degree of standardization is needed to promote effective implementation of countermeasures throughout the national transportation system.

- *On-going best practice surveys* - Finally, best practice surveys provide a means for compiling information on how various industries, both within and outside of the transportation community, approach security problems. While this study has assessed some of the most innovative and effective security practices, a continual re-evaluation must be made across public and private organizations, and the results compiled and disseminated.

Research & Development

There are three particular areas of concern regarding the vulnerability of the surface transportation system. First, the use of open architecture configurations in most information and communications systems supporting transportation leave them open to misuse and damage – either intentional or unintentional. Second, the increasing centralization of command and control activities in a decreasing number of operations centers brings improved efficiency, but at the cost of reducing the inherent redundancies in the transportation network that could help cushion the consequences of any disruption to it. Finally, there still remain physical vulnerabilities in the transportation infrastructure that could be exploited by those intent on disrupting its operations, particularly at the growing number of intermodal 'nodes' where passengers and freight are switched from one mode or link to another one to complete a journey.

Fortunately, possible solutions to many of these concerns can be found through research and development into improved countermeasures techniques, methods, materials and equipment. The results of these R&D activities can include improved means of identifying and measuring vulnerabilities and responding to security incidents, as well as better hardware and software for monitoring, detecting, mitigating and responding to such events. In fact, an effective improvement often requires upgrades to more than one of these elements.

Improved information security applications. While the information security countermeasures needed by the transportation community are not unique, the application of these measures to the transportation environment presents particular challenges. As noted by the PCCIP, transportation operators are not always active partners in the improvement of commercial data processing and communication systems. As a result, transportation is becoming more vulnerable through the extensive adoption of these systems.[13]

Security strategies must be developed for a wide variety of these applications, which can range from safety-critical operational control systems

to traveler information systems made readily accessible to the public. In particular, procedures and technology applications must be developed to ensure security of networks carrying information of varying levels of sensitivity. For example, the ITS Program is facilitating development and integration of a variety of technologies to improve emergency response capabilities, including automatic vehicle location systems, automated dispatching systems, geographic information systems and integrated emergency communications networks. These should all be adapted and evaluated for protection from terrorist or criminal activities. In addition, information security architectures, policy, procedures and software are needed for future data communications networks supporting highway and transit ITS systems, which may integrate or interconnect operational, administrative and public information systems. Further, these strategies must encompass both public and private information systems. For example, security of propriety data will be critical to gain private sector acceptance of planned Commercial Vehicle Information Systems and Networks (CVISN). The PCCIP has already recommended the development of security guidelines or standards for ITS to assist developers in designing security into their systems.

Improved analytical and decision support tools for operations, emergency response and resource allocation. Procedures and coordination plans for organizing emergency response should be established for major inter-city passenger carriers. Automated systems to support emergency decision-making could be very useful in this context, and should be investigated. Where possible, carriers should incorporate the capabilities which have been developed by the emergency response community.

In support of the Federal Aviation Administration, the Volpe Center developed a set of analytical models to determine the relative cost and effectiveness of alternative airport

---

13   *Ibid.*

security technology implementation strategies.[14] Similar models could be developed and applied to prioritize resource allocations and technology deployment plans on other modes of transportation such as rail or transit.

Evaluate current physical infrastructure vulnerabilities and develop means to improve survivability and reparability. Several scenarios revealed that remote segments of physical infrastructure, and the vehicles on those segments, can be vulnerable to serious terrorist threats, particularly those involving explosives. The hardening of these potential targets is a difficult problem, and requires research and development to determine the best and most cost-effective solutions. One possible approach could be to expand existing infrastructure data bases, such as those covering highway bridges and tunnels, to include information on vulnerabilities and reparability. Existing bridge management software could also be enhanced to model the impacts and costs associated with losing and replacing the structure.

Develop, demonstrate and implement new surveillance, monitoring and detection capabilities and improved operational procedures. The openness and high throughput required in busy facilities such as transit and inter-city passenger rail terminals precludes the kinds of passenger and luggage screening technologies and procedures routinely applied in airports. In general, less restrictive solutions must be applied. Fortunately, there are technology applications which can be tailored to these environments. For temporary high-threat situations, portable explosive screening technologies should be employed to check passengers, carry-on items and luggage. Other technologies which could be applied include improved magnetometers, bomb blankets and bags, blast resistant containers, and robots to move suspicious items. It is important to

---

[14]   *"Checked Baggage Screening (CBS) Analytical Model—User Manual,"* June 18, 1997.

evaluate this equipment in an operational setting before it is actually deployed.

Improved surveillance and monitoring technology is also needed for these environments. On-board video monitoring equipment has been tested by some transit authorities, for example, with a significant positive impact on crime and fraudulent injury claims. Improvements, such as digital data storage and remote "look-in" capabilities from control centers, could be effective in deterring, identifying or responding to terrorist and criminal actions. Continued development of this equipment is needed, as well as evaluation in the operational environment.

Video monitoring and closed circuit television systems also have potential to identify and document suspicious actions, but transit, passenger rail, and highway management agencies often lack the staff resources needed to monitor this equipment. "Smart" video monitoring systems are needed which would use pattern recognition and computational video technology to help identify abnormal events.

Continued research and development efforts are also needed to develop and evaluate countermeasures for the chemical and biological threat. Improved models of the behavior of chemical and biological agents in the subway tunnel, vehicle and station airflow environments must be developed. The Subway Environmental Simulation Model should be enhanced to represent both new and old transit facilities and include high volume sites such as multi-level stations. This model should be integrated with models such as the Consequences Assessment Tool Set, which can predict the migration of harmful agents into the adjacent community. In addition, these models should be validated through field testing using simulates in either actual transit facilities or controlled test sites, such as the Memorial Tunnel in West Virginia.

Both fixed and portable detection systems should be evaluated for the transportation environment, in coordination with the DoD

Technical Support Working Group and other federal agencies involved in evaluating Weapons of Mass Destruction countermeasures. Other equipment, such as Personal Protective Equipment (PPE) and decontamination systems, needs to be adapted to transportation applications and evaluated. DOT and transportation system operators should also participate in interagency consequence management exercises and red teaming dealing with chemical and biological attacks.

Additional forms of access control can be instituted to keep potential terrorists and criminals from reaching transportation targets easily. For example, electronic smart card photo IDs issued to employees can be used as card keys for access. Sensitive facilities at or near publicly accessible areas -- such as piers, bridges, terminals, and locks in urban areas or near recreational spots -- should have perimeter fences equipped with security lighting and a plan for human and/or canine patrols that can quickly be put into place during times of heightened tension. Intrusion detection sensors and card key systems could be installed at the most vulnerable points, such as control centers and equipment rooms. In some cases, physical security technologies will need to be adapted to withstand the particular environment (weather, salt water, etc.).

Standards and Guidelines

Develop standards for transportation crime data, data collection technology, regional databases. Nationwide, law enforcement agencies are mapping criminal occurrences to geographic locations to perform detailed spatial analysis to improve the effectiveness of directed patrol activities, to identify and "target harden" vulnerable areas, and to provide a more comprehensive, incident-based approach to crime reduction and police performance evaluation. However, some modes have been slow to adopt this technology for a number of reasons.

Work needs to be performed to develop a model

crime data collection process for all transportation environments, and to integrate GIS technology into this process. Training or workshops should be provided to disseminate this model process and to strengthen data collection and analysis skills.

Risk assessment and modeling handbook for transportation operators. Risk assessment is a crucial security loss prevention function. This process is complex, and data is not always available. A set of guidelines or a handbook on how to perform security risk assessments in transportation environments (for both criminal activity and terrorism) could greatly improve the awareness and capabilities of the industry. This should be coupled with training initiatives. The handbook should also be incorporated into established transportation security initiatives.

On-Going Best Practice Surveys

Compile best practices for transportation security. Much can be learned by evaluating practices already in place in the industry. This study has identified some of the most innovative and effective current practices, but continuing assessments are needed in all modes to track evolving security practices and to address changing threats. The information collected should be disseminated through cooperative public/private efforts using the communications mechanisms described in the following section.

Stage 3: Implementing Solutions

The third class of countermeasure initiatives involves those that facilitate implementation of solutions aimed at mitigating vulnerabilities to terrorist and other security threats.

- *Regulations, legislation, and government roles* - These activities deal with the actions to be taken by government agencies, such as coordination between agencies and with the private sector, and the potential development of legislation or regulations to improve the security and integrity of the nation's transportation infrastructure.

- *Training, workshops, and exercises* – These activities involve dissemination of information to improve the awareness and capabilities of those responsible for transportation security in both the public and private sectors.

- *Demonstrations and evaluations* – To facilitate the development and implementation of countermeasures that are effective in the transportation environment, demonstrations and evaluations of technologies and procedures are needed, and the results must be disseminated to all potential users.

Regulation, Legislation & Government Roles

Modified roles and responsibilities. Figure 3 shows a number of new organizations and roles that were recommended by the PCCIP to improve infrastructure security. These roles include both public and private entities, and would be instrumental in facilitating improved security for surface transportation. The many professional organizations and associations supporting the surface transportation industry should be involved in these efforts, as appropriate. In addition, the OST Office of Intelligence and Security and the various modal administrations should all participate in these activities.

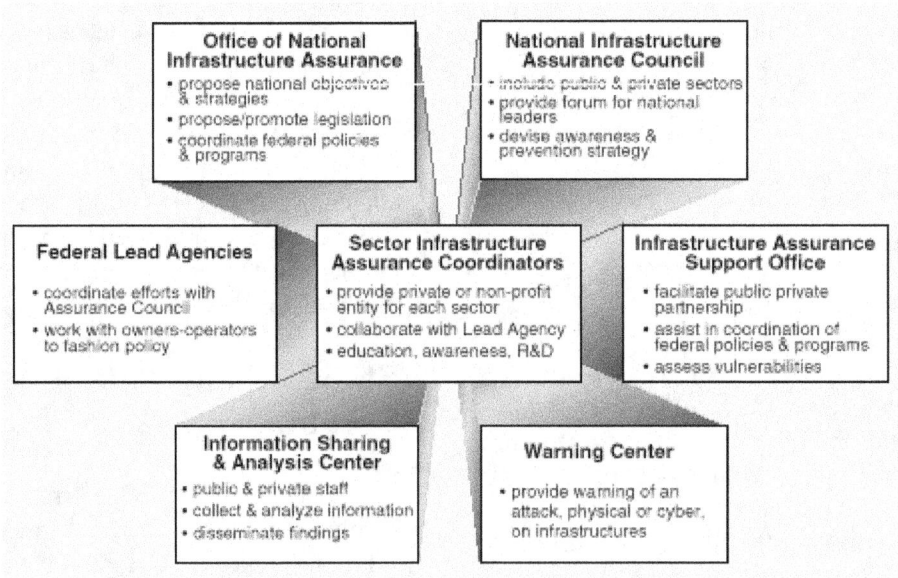

Figure 3. Roles for Improving Infrastructure Security

As recommended by the PCCIP, the DOT should consider:

- Establishing a central office for infrastructure assurance and coordination with government and industry organizations.

- Developing joint response and recovery plans with government and industry.

- Establishing and testing an improved information sharing and dissemination process.

- Reviewing proposed legislation for adherence to assurance policies.

Training, Workshops, and Exercises

The need for more training has been highlighted for many types of vulnerabilities identified in this study. Specific recommendations include:

Surface transportation terrorism and security training. In support of the Coast Guard, the Federal Law Enforcement Training Center (FLETC) has developed a Maritime Security Training Course. Similar training should be developed for the other modes. This could be a joint effort between FLETC, DOT and the various professional organizations addressing transportation security. The course could incorporate transit security and emergency response curricula developed by FTA and the RSPA Transportation Safety Institute. The facilities of the Association of American Railroads in Pueblo, CO could also provide valuable assistance.

Promoting educational curricula. The PCCIP recommended that the federal sector should promote and support development of undergraduate and graduate level programs in security, particularly information security, with particular focus on critical transportation issues.

Employee and patron vigilance. Because of the open environment of surface transportation

stations and facilities, countermeasures must be more oriented to people-based procedures than to technology. One very effective approach is the concept of employee and patron vigilance. For example, as a result of an employee vigilance and passenger awareness program in Chicago's Union Station, theft was reduced by over 60% in one year. Similar success has been reported by New York City Transit and New York Port Authority. The video tape for employees developed by the Long Island Railroad after a shooting on-board a commuter train is a good example of the type of mechanism which could be used to promote this concept. Pamphlets, signs and radio announcements were used to increase passengers awareness in New York and following the terrorist bombings in Paris subway stations. In addition to deterring and detecting crime and terrorist activities, these approaches can constructively involve patrons in proactive campaigns to address security concerns. Because of the limitations of technology in open environments, these approaches may be critical to combat the vulnerabilities in passenger rail and transit described in Section Four.

Handbook for transit risk assessments. Risk assessment is a crucial security loss prevention function. Performance of this process is currently required by recent rail fixed guideway State Safety Oversight legislation (for heavy and light rail systems). Yet, this process is complex and data is not always available. A set of guidelines or a handbook on how to perform security risk assessments (for both criminal activity and terrorism) could greatly improve the capabilities of the transit industry.

Demonstrations and Evaluations

Many types of countermeasures should be demonstrated and evaluated as part of initial implementation in the surface transportation operating environment. This process could be facilitated, and should be at least partially funded, by DOT as part of a "Security Technology and Practices Demonstration Program." Successful demonstrations would assist the transportation industry in specifying, purchasing and implementing these technologies, and would guide private industry to developing these technologies with security in mind.

Among the highest priority, in terms of vulnerabilities and available information are both information security and physical security countermeasures for major transportation facilities and systems. Examples of these include: Intelligent Transportation System (ITS), transit and railroad traffic management centers; SCADA pipeline systems; and applications such as video monitoring and detection systems, integrated communications, and electronic data interchange (EDI).

APPENDIX A - BEST PRACTICES

Introduction

Terrorism mitigation measures in this country historically have focused more on aviation than on surface transportation. Recent incidents, however, have caused a growing awareness concerning the likely impacts of a successful attack on surface modes. Attacks against transportation and transportation infrastructures accounted for nearly one third of the international terrorist attacks reported by the U.S. State Department in 1996. Further, since 1991, surface transportation modes have increasingly been the target of terrorism; public transportation alone has been the target of 20 to 35 percent of worldwide terrorist attacks.

As a result, all of the (surface) modes under study have initiated practices to improve terrorism response capabilities. Over the past decade, in particular, transportation operators have assumed greater responsibility for terrorism mitigation and response. Each mode has responded to its own specific security and terrorist history, and has developed and implemented security practices that are consistent with its actual and assessed vulnerabilities. There are, however, similarities in these activities across the surface transportation modes and intermodal facilities.

This chapter summarizes these best practices that constitute the initial building blocks for improving surface transportation security nationwide.

Most Significant Vulnerabilities to be Addressed with Best Practices

Both passenger and freight modes are considered in this report. Passenger modes - transit, rail, highway, and maritime (cruise ships) - are more vulnerable to incidents that result in high casualties, and have, therefore, been more likely to be targets of attack. While these events may not result in sustained, long-term disruptions to the regional or national transportation system, they have the capability to injure or kill large numbers of people and to instill fear in the travelling public. Passenger terminal and facilities are vulnerable to small quantities of explosives, large quantities of explosives, and chemical or biological releases – all of which can result in high casualties. Acts of extreme violence, such as passenger shootings, hijacking, and hostage/barricade situations can also result in casualties and heightened fear levels.

Attacks against freight modes of surface transportation (rail, highway, maritime, and pipeline) have the potential for major economic disruption and, depending on the nature of the attack, could also produce human casualties.

Intermodal connections and transfer points are among the most vulnerable elements of the surface transportation infrastructure. Intermodal passenger terminals are densely populated and may serve passengers from several modes. Intermodal freight transfers provide criminal opportunities for theft and smuggling, and also could become "bottlenecks" in the event of a major incident.

Best Practices

Since a large scale terrorist event or act of extreme violence is likely to require assistance from a number of emergency management agencies at all levels of government, best practices presented in this chapter are organized according to the Federal Emergency Management Agency's (FEMA) four generally recognized phases of emergency management:

Mitigation - Activities performed in advance to reduce or eliminate threats.

Preparedness - Activities performed in advance to develop response capabilities.

Response - Activities performed after an event occurs to save lives, protect property, and stabilize the situation.

Recovery - Activities performed after a crisis has been stabilized to return all systems to normal.

Each of the categories is explained below, with examples of best practices from all passenger and freight surface modes as well as intermodalism.

Mitigation

In the *Mitigation Phase*, problem identification and hazard analysis provide crucial assessments to guide the development of design criteria, the selection of transportation equipment and vehicles, and the modification of facilities. Mitigation activities ensure the selection and documentation of those features that offer the most effective mitigation capabilities, which meet all federal, state, and local requirements and which successfully incorporate industry standards and advancements. Activities performed during the mitigation phase support agency-wide efforts to ensure compliance with selected design criteria.

Mitigation activities can be classified into the following four categories, examples of which follow:

- Facility and vehicle design criteria;
- Hazard analysis (site specific threat and vulnerability identification and resolution);
- Identifying technology; and
- Integrating technology into existing operations.

Research for this first phase of "best practices" identification indicates that each mode of transportation (be it freight or passenger) is actively engaging in practices that are designed to maintain, or in some cases increase, the integrity of the respective systems while achieving some degree of increased efficiency. Many safety and security improvements are being implemented across the modes. Rail agencies, in recognition of the impact of a security breech or critical incident, are implementing system back-up plans, local track inspections, and officer deployment in an attempt to safeguard rail systems from terrorist activity. New technologies such as GPS, AEI, and EDI are allowing rail and maritime industries, in addition to trucking companies, to track shipments of cargo.

The use of design techniques to avert criminal activity is becoming more popular in each modal industry. Transit agencies, generally more susceptible to criminal behavior, are employing many new techniques in an effort to "design out crime" while maintaining the efficiency of a service that transports 8 billion persons each year. These new techniques, coupled with the growing integration of security technology are providing transit systems with the means to reduce system vulnerability to acts of terrorism and extreme violence.

Facility and Vehicle Design Criteria

Implementation of CPTED Techniques. Research demonstrates that certain elements of the transportation environment can have an impact on the level and types of crime that occur on a given system.[15] Failure to recognize and incorporate crime prevention features during system planning may result in higher than anticipated crime rates, elevated passenger fear, and expensive system modifications in response to critical incidents.

There are two key approaches used in designing and maintaining facilities and vehicles; these are Crime Prevention Through Environmental Design (CPTED) and Situational Crime Prevention (SCP). While CPTED is invaluable in the initial design of transportation facilities, SCP offers many advantages during the life cycle of the transportation system. SCP provides a scientific framework for practical use. This framework relies on a standard action research methodology consisting of five sequential stages:

- Collecting data relevant to the specific crime problem;
- Analyzing the specific situational conditions that facilitate such criminal activity;
- Analyzing the costs and benefits associated with methods of deterring such criminal activity;
- Implementing the most promising countermeasure; and
- Monitoring and evaluating the results of the particular implementation plan.

Specific CPTED techniques can include, but are not limited to, the following:

- Removing niches, corners and darkness;
- Increased lighting;
- Target hardening;
- Appointment of full-time managers;
- Employee access control; and
- Bomb-resistant litter containers.

It is important to recognize that the utility of architectural design principles is not limited to the planning life cycle phase. In the transit environment specifically, older systems, such as

[15] Clarke, Ronald V. Preventing Mass Transit Crime, Vol. 6. Criminal Justice Press, New York, 1996, p. 2.

New York City's Port Authority Bus Terminal (PABT) and Massachusetts Bay Transportation Authority (MBTA), have effectively incorporated Crime Prevention Through Environmental Design (CPTED) criteria.

In addition to the renovations by PABT and MBTA, other transit agencies have used CPTED principles for preventative measures. The design, maintenance, and management of WMATA provides an excellent example of "designing out crime." WMATA employed CPTED techniques by designing the system with the following attributes:

- Elimination of dark corners to alleviate criminal activity;
- Enhanced lighting to remove shadows (sometimes responsible for patron fear);
- Installation of CCTV's to provide surveillance and greater visibility; and
- Training transit police and personnel to deter criminal activity.

Establish Safety Design Criteria. One way to ensure that mitigation measures are incorporated into transit agency design, construction, and maintenance is to develop design criteria that establishes minimum acceptable levels for health and industrial safety, and which provide protection from fire, smoke, explosion, natural disasters, and public panic/civil disturbances. These criteria provide general guidance, and identify the major needs of fire and life safety in the following areas:

- Station facilities;
- Vehicles;
- Guideway facilities;
- Vehicle yard and maintenance facilities;
- Communications; and
- Power.

An example of this approach to mitigation is the development by San Francisco's Bay Area Rapid Transit District (BART) of Facilities Safety Criteria to provide minimum safety requirements for the design of BART's facilities. The following criteria were established to achieve system safety by eliminating, minimizing, or controlling hazards through analysis, review, and design selection:

- Design for Hazard Elimination. Provisions were made in all initial designs for the elimination of hazards. If the identified hazards could not be eliminated, then the hazards were controlled through alternative designs.
- Safety Devices. Hazards that could not be eliminated or controlled through design were controlled through the use of fixed, automatic, or other protective safety design features. Provisions were made for periodic functional checks of safety devices.
- Warning Devices. When neither design nor safety devices could effectively eliminate or control an identified hazard, devices were used to detect the hazard and to generate an adequate warning signal to provide for operating personnel/public reaction.
- Procedures and Training. Where it was impossible to eliminate or adequately control a hazard through design or through the use of safety and warning devices, procedures and training were used to control the hazard.

Increase Capacity of Bridges. Bridges are key infrastructure elements because they act as bottlenecks to the flow of traffic and because they are relatively limited in number (providing less redundancy than do roadways). This situation is aggravated by the fact that many of the nation's bridges are in poor condition. Currently, efforts are underway to improve the condition of bridges, increasing their capacity, and, therefore, addressing this vulnerability:

- High performance materials are used to retrofit existing highway structures to increase capacity or eliminate deficiencies; and
- Imbedding sensors in bridges to monitor bridge performance.

Information Technology Systems (ITS) Security. To address vulnerabilities of data that are critical to the security and integrity of ITS systems, a variety of methods, such as access control to centralized computer facilities and computer security measures (e.g., firewalls), are used. Also, routine backups of data and redundant (backup) computer hardware further protect these systems.

Safety Improvements. The Federal Railroad Administration released reports in November 1997, citing gains in safety on both CSX Transportation and Union Pacific. The reports were issued after intensive safety investigations on both railroads. The FRA's report on CSX identifies safety improvements in five critical areas: the transport of hazardous materials, motive power and equipment, operating practices, signal and train control systems, and track.

The FRA said that the railroad and rail labor have already acted upon many of its findings, initiating over 250 corrective action projects system-wide. FRA, CSXT and rail labor unions have formed 16 action teams to: jointly resolve safety concerns; perform training; conduct a fatigue/rest pilot project; and provide new computer software that enables employees to access train line-up information. In the report on Union Pacific, the FRA identified five areas where the railroad and its labor organizations are taking steps to address safety concerns: culture, staffing, fatigue, dispatching, and safety training.[16] Many of these initiatives could have positive impacts on the railroads' ability to address security issues.

Positive Train Control (PTC) System. Positive train control systems may be less vulnerable to attack due to their spread spectrum communications and inherent redundancy and protection features. The AAR, Federal Railroad Administration and Illinois Department of Transportation have a joint positive train control demonstration project on 123 miles of Union Pacific track between Chicago and Springfield, Ill. The project tests interoperability with other train control systems now being demonstrated. the AAR Board of Directors voted to invest $20 million in the project over the next four years.

---

[16] Train It! Volume V, Number 4, 3/5/98.

These funds will be combined with future appropriations and the $15 million already available to FRA and IDOT. The FRA funding comes from the Next Generation High Speed Rail Program.

The project involves the use of the Nationwide Differential Global Positioning System to automatically locate each train, computers onboard each locomotive, and a digital radio network to automatically link each locomotive to the UP's Harriman Control Center in Omaha. The onboard computer is designed to automatically monitor the train's speed, assuring that locomotive engineers don't exceed permitted speeds, don't pass red signals, and don't operate beyond track limits approved by the control center. The system is also designed to provide enhanced protection to track maintenance workers. The ultimate goal of the system is to enable flexible block operation, in which the control center moves the maximum possible number of trains, safely, by permitting operations more closely spaced than permitted by the current wayside signal system.

FRA Administrator Jolene Molitoris praised the railroad industry's commitment to the project, calling it a reasonable step to test new technologies that hold great promise for improving transportation. The FRA also said it would support a joint effort with rail labor organizations to assure training in these applications of new technology. The AAR will use this stretch of track as a PTC test bed to determine the validity of the proposed full PTC technology and to assess its potential safety and productivity gains.[17]

Locomotive and Car Design Standards. Industry and governmental equipment design standards assure the safety of tank cars, locomotives, and nuclear vaults mitigate possible human and environmental losses.

Backup Plans. In response to potential cyber threats, railroads have instituted measures to protect their operating centers. They are also instituting competent back-up systems that allow

for rapid reinstallation of operating systems and databases, and have outlined strategies to assure early restoration of service after a successful attack.

Disaster Response and Federal Aid. The railroad industry has set in place Emergency Response Procedures (ERPs) throughout the major divisional or regional locations. Various terminals and control centers are their official response coordination offices. The ERP are part of their overall operational plans filed with the FRA in Washington, D.C.

Container Seal Improvements. High-value containerized cargo is being secured with bolt or cable barrier locking systems, which tie a container's two central locking bars in such a way that even if a barrier seal on the handle is removed, or the handle itself is detached from the lock rod, it is impossible to open the doors in the normal manner. There are several such products now available. Models use either a reusable pick- and-drill-resistant locking cylinder or a single-use disposable unit, suitable for areas where recovery of reusable locks is difficult. Container seal tape that changes color or appearance when opened also makes theft or tampering more difficult to conceal. Furthermore, in order to reduce losses, insurance companies and shippers are now pressuring shipping lines to secure containers with heavy-duty barrier seals, even to the extent of making this a condition of insurance.[18]

Physical Security. Ports and port facilities employ a variety of measures to control access. In addition to fencing, lighting, and guardhouses, some facilities employ more sophisticated technology such as electronic container tags and closed circuit television.

Access Control Systems (ACS). Some automated gatehouse facilities are using Access Control Systems to monitor traffic flow in and out of facilities. These complexes use information systems to match cargo, paperwork,

---

[17] Train IT! Vilume V, Number 3, 2/19/98.

[18] "Fraud, Hijacking and Theft of Valuables," Patrick Barco, Chair, Container Security, Canadian Bureau of Marine Underwriters, www.webcom.com/cbmu

trucks, and drivers at exit points, and are designed to reduce the illegal movement of goods out of facilities. The Seagirt Marine Terminal at the Port of Baltimore uses a computerized gate complex that serves as the nerve center for the terminal. Seagirt's automated system consolidates the steps necessary to generate the Trailer Interchange Report (TIR). When trucks enter the terminal, an electronic sign-bridge over 13 of the 14 inbound lanes directs the drivers to the appropriate lane, where a remote intercom system allows them to quickly exchange information with clerks in the gatehouse. For export traffic, trucks are directed to one of four lanes with built-in scales. While the driver supplies the clerk with the necessary information, the container's weight is automatically input into the clerk's computer. The driver then pulls under the gatehouse canopy, where a terminal mechanic inspects the container and chassis for any damage. Should any be found, the Seagirt computer prohibits the clerk from reassigning the equipment until it has been repaired. The driver then receives the TIR and is released into the terminal. The process for import loads is essentially the same. The clerk verifies the driver's information and that the container has received all the appropriate releases. The clerk then issues the TIR, informing the driver where the container is stored. After picking up the container, the driver goes to one of the five outbound lanes, where a security check and final inspection are performed.[19]

Pre-programmed Closed-loop Controls. Pipeline companies use start-up sequences for pumps and valve lineup operations that are programmed into the system to protect the equipment and to facilitate its operation. Remote devices consist of Remote Terminal Units or Programmable Logic Controllers that interface with transducers and output devices and execute control commands issued by the SCADA system, or are optionally controlled locally by an operator at the remote location. They are typically microprocessor-based and are programmed to perform closed-loop control of a piece of equipment or process.

Read-only Data Servers. Some pipeline companies have the real-time data server made read-only to the user. This provides an additional measure of security to prevent unauthorized access by internal users. The real-time data server is a processor used to provide data plant-wide for engineering and other uses. The purpose of the server is to reduce the processing load on the applications processor and to isolate the intranet user from the systems used by the operators.

Hazard Analysis (threat and vulnerability identification and resolution)

Risk Assessment. The performance of risk assessments by transportation agencies aids the agency in the identification of system vulnerabilities. The results of a risk assessment assist security officials in making critical decisions concerning the allocation of resources, such as where to harden targets, change procedures, and detail officers. Some of the methods used include:

- Terrorism and quasi-terrorism specific risk assessments;
- Risk assessments performed as a part of the overall system design process; and
- Security inspections performed in the normal course of police or private security operations.

Threat Identification. Once a risk assessment has been completed, interviewed officials recommended documenting potential terrorist threats to the high-risk areas of the system. This documentation enables system vulnerabilities to be clearly identified and prioritized.

Several methods may be used to identify these threats, including:

- Analysis of historical data and application of this information to the development of

---

[19] Port of Baltimore web site, http://www.mpa.state.md.us/

different attack scenarios against the
system;

- Review of threat checklists developed by
the agency or obtained through other
sources such as consultants;
- Judgment of transit agency senior
personnel (based on experience and
knowledge of system vulnerabilities); and
- Use of formal analyses, including
Preliminary Threat Analysis (PTA) and
Fault Tree Analysis (FTA).

The Long Island Rail Road (LIRR) Police
Department, in their *Security System Selections
and Surveys*, outline their extensive threat and
vulnerability analysis and countermeasures to
address security concerns. The document
outlines their approach to system design and
access control systems, as well as closed circuit
television and intrusion detectors.

Vulnerability Assessments. The Transit Bureau
and NYC Transit have together identified
specific areas of the subway system that are
vulnerable to terrorist attack, and have prepared
a booklet identifying them. The booklet has
been given to Transit Bureau commands for
their use so that heightened patrol and security
activity may be deployed to the vulnerable
areas.[20]

Tunnel, Track and Room Inspections. New
York City Police Department's Transit Bureau
deploys track certified personnel routinely, each
month, to walk through tunnels in key areas to
conduct inspections. These sweeps are designed
to prevent and detect the presence of explosives
and chemical/biological weapons. Further,
rooms that have been identified as a possible
security risk are properly secured by NYC
Transit Personnel.[21]

Collection of Cargo Theft Data. One industry
attempt to collect and disseminate cargo theft
data is the TIPS II database system, a creation of
the Transportation Loss Prevention and Security

Council of the American Trucking Association
(ATA). In addition, some state and local law
enforcement agencies have developed systems to
compile cargo security data for their region.

Crime Reduction Focus. Some regional multi-
jurisdictional entities are focused on reducing
crime. In response to extensive problems with
organized crime in the New York/New Jersey
port district, the Waterfront Commission of New
York Harbor was established in 1953. Today,
the Waterfront Commission has broad
investigative, licensing, regulatory and police
authority over piers and terminals in the port
district. It investigates criminal activity,
registers and licenses longshoremen, stevedore
companies, hiring agents, pier superintendents
and pier guards, regulates and monitors dock
employment, and exercises broad police
authority.[22]

***Multi-disciplinary Cargo Theft Task Force
Programs.*** These programs, involving local and
regional police organizations, are focused on
reducing cargo crime in high-theft areas. A $1.1
million pilot program began in FY97 in south
Florida. This program has been successful, and
additional funding is being sought for New
York/New Jersey for FY98, and also for
Southern California.[23]

Directed Law Enforcement Operations.
Undercover law enforcement operations are
being directed at specific problem areas.
Operation conducted by the FBI's San Jose-
based high-tech crime squad -- Operation
"Dragon Teeth" in 1994, Operation
"Chiptryster" in 1995, Operation "Westchips" in
February, 1996 and Operation "Bytes Dust" in
April, 1996 have put a significant dent in
premises thefts, particularly in California. Those
arrested in these roundups have also been linked
to home invasions, money laundering and
counterfeiting activities, illegal gambling,

[20] Donohue, Kenneth J. *Terrorism: Real Life Experiences,
The American Perspective*, FTA, 1996.
[21] Donohue, Kenneth J. *Terrorism: Real Life Experiences,
The American Perspective*, FTA, 1996.

[22] Policing Transportation Facilities, p. 34
[23] The Current Cargo Crime Situation, A Presentation
at the US Capitol, Edward V. Badolato, National
Cargo Security Council, Chairman

fictitious business frauds, as well as a myriad of drug and weapons violations.[24]

Employee Background Checks. The Waterfront Commission of New York Harbor actively monitors port employment, providing licenses for longshoremen, checkers, hiring agents, pier superintendents, pier guards, stevedore companies, and telecommunication systems controllers.[25]

Provide Shippers with Up-to-Date Information. Insurers are taking an active role in working to reduce losses. For example, CIGNA Insurance Companies provide CIGNA Ports of the World, a guide to aid traders and shippers. The guide includes current port conditions, guidelines to assure secure cargo transportation, and recommendations to minimize cargo loss and damage.

National Bridge Inventory. The National Bridge Inventory is a tool currently used to catalogue the state of repair of the nation's bridges, and to a lesser extent tunnels. While improvements can be made to the information contained in the inventory in order to understand security vulnerabilities, the existence of a catalogue of all bridges is a useful model for other modes.

Identifying Technology

Physical Security Technology. Many transit agencies have taken steps to reduce system vulnerability to acts of terrorism and extreme violence using physical security equipment. The following physical security equipment is used in the transportation industry:

- Closed Circuit Television (CCTV). Constant monitoring; video recording capability, alarm-activated recording; monitored safety zones.

- Intrusion-detection alarms. Electro-mechanical, microwave, ultrasonic.

- Access control. Electronic access control systems; employee ID badges; magnetic-card key; employee sign-in procedures; work order procedures; fences and gates; locks; vaults.

- Communications. Radio; public address system; emergency station and rail car phones; train annunciator systems; and silent alarms.

- Blast resistant litter containers. Specialized materials for the construction of trashcans.

- Vehicle barriers. Concrete barriers for placement to protect system.

Installation of Closed Circuit Televisions. The use of CCTV and Closed Circuit Video Recording (CCVR) have become increasingly popular in the security industry. Both forms of surveillance technology allow for real-time monitoring and/or video recording, thus providing station users a means by which they could view system operations and suspicious activities. The reasons behind employing CCTV and CCVR technology may vary from station to station, but several applications (see Table A-1) are generally consistent with this form of surveillance technology.

---

[24] "High Tech Cargo Theft," A Presentation at the US Capitol, MaryLu Korkuch, Executive Director, Technology Theft Prevention Foundation, April 9, 1996
[25] Policing Transportation Facilities, p. 35

Table A-1. CCTV Applications

Application	Description
Monitoring of Revenue Facilities	Use of CCTV to view stations/terminals. Camera feeds may be directed to a centralized (dispatch) location or to a localized monitoring area (e.g., Station Agent's Booth)
Monitoring of Vehicles	Use of CCTV to monitor activities on rail vehicles; to record accidents/incidents; to promote patron perception of security
Incident Management	Camera feeds to dispatch room, central control, or station manager's booth to enable personnel monitoring CCTV to call staff to respond to an incident; to enhance accurate description of incident; to provide a video record
Legal Evidence	Continuous, random, or emergency monitoring of facilities or vehicles for use as evidence in legal proceedings
Customer Service	Visibility of passengers (e.g., at customer assistance phones) to assist patrons more efficiently; to identify patrons with problems; to identify mechanical failures
Crowd Control	Use of cameras to alert dispatch of crowd control problems on platforms or in other areas of facilities
Security of Problem Areas	Use of CCTV in difficult-to-patrol areas such as elevators or parking lots to deter criminal activity; to support police operations; to enhance incident response
Visibility for Operators	CCTV and monitors are used as a safety feature, providing rail operators with additional visibility of platform areas prior to door closure or vehicle pull-in/pull-out
Special Police Operations	Portable or mounted cameras used to assist undercover police officers in observing facilities; identifying perpetrators; documenting activities
Risk Management	Verification of insurance claims against the RFGS, typically resulting from (alleged) accidents
Vehicle Routing	Use of CCTV cameras on bridges or highways to identify traffic patterns, accidents, and delay patterns
Non-revenue Areas	CCTV utilized for monitoring non-revenue areas such as cash counting areas, power sub-stations, storage rooms, and administrative facilities

BART is installing a fiber optic CCTV system for stations along its new rapid transit lines (most CCTV networks in transit use coaxial cable). This technology will utilize a distribution system that connects all CCTV cameras through a Local Area Network (LAN) so that any location on the LAN can access real-time video from any camera on the network. Signals are transmitted to the LAN over fiber optic cables. This system will be connected directly to BART's Central Control, with feeds available at the individual stations as well. This CCTV surveillance system will allow a dispatcher at a remote console to assess a given situation and dispatch the appropriate personnel to any incident. In an emergency situation, multiple BART officers can be informed of the situation by CCTV assessment. Videotape can also be recorded off any camera on the LAN.

Screening and Sensor Technology. Many transit agencies are now evaluating security technologies developed for other industries such as the military. Following the sarin gas attacks on the Tokyo subway system, a few rail agencies in the U.S. have begun to consider using chemical and biological sensors in vehicles and stations. Washington Metro was to have started the initial testing of chemical sensors in late 1997. In addition to the new chemical and biological sensors, other technology being evaluated includes:

- Access control systems that incorporate biometric verification devices;
- Hardened containers to reduce the impact of explosive devices (luggage containers, trash receptacles); and

- Software programs that incorporate video images of real and simulated scenarios for transit police training programs.[26]

Integrating Technology into Existing Operations

Access Control Devices. Over the last decade, electronic Access Control Systems (ACS) technology has improved significantly in efficiency and reliability. Recent innovations include:

- Improvements in off-the-shelf distribution database software;
- The introduction of the micro controller (enables fault tolerance and independent decision-making for access denial and alarm triggers; and
- The development of miniature micro controllers that can be housed in the card reader panel and do not require separate wall panels and wiring.

In addition, CCTV and "smart" building management systems have revolutionized ACS capabilities. Software innovations allow electronic ACS technologies to integrate with Building Management Systems, Fire Detection and Suppression Systems, and CCTV Surveillance Systems. There are three basic electronic ACS devices:

- Proximity, Smart Card or Magnetic Swipe Card Readers;
- Alphanumeric Code Entry Systems; and
- Personal Feature Identification (PFI)/Biometric Systems.[27]

Intrusion Alarms on Emergency Exits. Intrusion alarms have been installed in 13 emergency exits in the New York subway system. These alarms are equipped with audio alarms, flashing lights, and a verbal annunciator which warns intruders that police have been notified of their unauthorized entry. The alarms are connected, via dedicated lines, to alarms and printers in NYPD Transit Bureau commands.[28]

Use of Advanced Computer Systems and Software to Monitor and Track Shipments. The Ports of Seattle and Tacoma use an EDI system called LINX to optimize movement of goods through the port. The Port of New York and New Jersey uses the Advanced Cargo Expediting System (ACES) to provide shipment status and location information. Information provided includes arrival notices from ocean carriers, delivery orders from customs house brokers, cargo status replies from marine terminals, and electronic bookings from freight forwarders to ocean carriers.[29]

Use of Automatic Equipment Identification (AEI) Technology to Track Containers in Terminals. AEI technology uses bar codes and bar code scanners with radios to transfer real-time data on shipping containers and/or vehicle locations. Many carriers are using AEI technology. Uses include container identification, chassis management, automatic container/trailer weighing, gate access control and intermodal movement operations. Benefits include accurate data entry, faster location of containers in terminals, and reduced workforce requirements.[30]

Use of Global Positioning System (GPS) to Track Shipment Locations Intransit. Many companies currently use GPS systems to track the worldwide movement of their ships and provide customers with accurate status and arrival information. Ultimately, GPS technology could be used (most likely in combination with other technologies such as AEI) to track the movement of individual containers from the time they are loaded until they reach their final destination.

---

[26] Michael G. Dinning. "Technology and Innovation in Transit Security," *Transit Policing,* Vol. 7, n. 1 Spring 1997.

[27] Boyd, M. Annabelle and Maier, M. Patricia. State Safety Oversight Security Handbook, USDOT, FTA, 1997.

[28] Donohue, Kenneth J. *Terrorism: Real Life Experiences, The American Perspective,* FTA, 1996.

[29] Intermodal Freight Transportation, 3rd Edition, Gerhardt Muller, p. 190

[30] Intermodal Freight Transportation, 3rd Edition, Gerhardt Muller, p. 192

Tracking of Goods to Prevent Theft. Theft and pilferage are common problems in the shipment of goods. The first step in preventing such crimes is to pinpoint the location of goods at each step in their movement from origin to destination. Certain firms (such as Federal Express and United Parcel Service) have developed reliable tracking systems that have this type of security functionality.

Electronic Air Brake Systems. Amtrak ordered Electronic Air brake Systems (EABS) from Rockwell to equip eight locomotives, 64 auto carriers and 43 coaches for Amtrak's Auto Train. EABS brakes were developed, and are manufactured, by TSM, Inc., Kansas City, Mo., a subsidiary of Rockwell Collins of Cedar Rapids, Iowa. Installation of the new brake systems will be completed in the Spring of 1998.

Greg Gagarin, assistant general manager, Amtrak Mechanical Standards and Compliance, said the new brakes will help Amtrak meet increased customer demand by operating longer trains as well as improve train handling and control through more efficient braking.

EABS is an electronically controlled braking system for trains that applies rail car brakes uniformly throughout a train so that it stops as a unit rather than permitting cars to bump each other during the stopping process, as with old pneumatic braking systems.[31]

Another railroad, Southern Company, has ordered more than 2,500 sets of EABS worth more than $7 million. Earlier this year, Southern Company ordered 250 coal cars equipped with EABS brakes. The first train entered service on the Burlington Northern Santa Fe railroad between the Powder River Basin coal fields in Wyoming and Southern Company's Miller Steam Plant in Birmingham, Ala., on Feb. 1, 1997. More than 500 EABS equipped cars will have been delivered to Southern Company by the end of 1997.

Electronic brakes permit railroads to maintain safety margins while operating trains at higher speeds, thus increasing capacity. EABS provides improved safety and train handling, and up to 70 percent shorter stopping distances for trains compared to conventional air brake systems.[32] This capability may improve the ability of the train crew to react to security incidents.

Preparedness

During the ***Preparedness Phase***, transportation operators identify operating policies and procedures for the rapid mobilization of transportation and public safety personnel in response to an act of terrorism or extreme violence. Successful preparedness ensures the selection of optimal policies and procedures, their documentation in clear and widely distributed plans, their integration into Standard Operating Procedures (SOPs) wherever possible, and their effective implementation through comprehensive and effective training programs and drills.

Preparedness activities can be classified into the following five categories, examples of which follow:

- Obtaining executive and management support;
- Planning;
- Coordination;
- Development of incident management tools; and
- Training and drills.

Commitment from management to address the preparedness deemed necessary to respond to an incident is integral to any agency preparing for possible terrorist activity. Each mode is developing, to some degree, plans that will address security, safety, and contingency efforts. The Office of Intelligence and Security recently published a pamphlet that discussed the importance of advance planning for special events, and the ways each mode might be affected in the event of a terrorist incident.

---

[31] Train It! Volume V, Number 2, 2/5/98

[32] Train It! Volume IV, Number 21, 10/30/97

Similarly, many modal agencies have coordinated with local, state, and federal agencies to develop plans that will address roles and responsibilities during critical incidents. Nowhere is this more apparent than in public transportation, where transit agencies have entered into extensive agreements with other agencies, generally in the form of Memoranda of Understanding, coordinating planning and response efforts. It is during the preparedness phase that many agencies have trained personnel on safety and security issues and concerns.

Obtaining Executive and Management Support

Obtain Executive and Management Support. Before initiating significant efforts to enhance the transit agency's capabilities in mitigating and responding to acts of terrorism and extreme violence, transit police departments generally seek active support from top management.

According to transit agencies, a clear and widely distributed Terrorism Policy Statement from the General Manager or Executive Director can provide the necessary support to develop enhanced terrorism prevention and response programs by:

- Emphasizing the importance of addressing the threat of terrorism/extreme violence;
- Designating authority for the police/security department or some other operational unit to develop and implement necessary plans and procedures and to purchase technology; and
- Demonstrating management commitment of resources and personnel.

Obtain the endorsement of top management for these programs:

- Information, including assessments from the FBI and other intelligence organizations, detailing the extent of the threat to mass transit;
- Reports from other transit agencies detailing their anti- and counter-terrorism initiatives; and

- Media reports concerning acts of terrorism/extreme violence at home and abroad.

Office of Emergency Management. New York City Mayor Giuliani, by executive order, established the Office of Emergency Management with responsibility for interagency and intergovernmental coordination of NYC's response to emergencies. This job includes the development of all emergency plans, training, preparation, and response to all emergencies. The OEM is directly responsible for the coordination of all emergency services but does not govern their operational activities. The OEM was born out of the necessity for clear command and control during complicated emergency situations when the division of responsibility can become difficult. Under this plan, for example, if an explosion were to occur on a railway track and the NYFD were the first emergency service to respond, it would take the operational lead. However, should a suspicious object be found to have caused the blast, the NYPD would assume control of the situation until it was satisfied that no crime had been committed or until its investigations had been completed. Once the NYPD had declared the area safe, the control might switch back to the NYFD or the NYC Transit as circumstances dictate.

Carrier Management Emphasis on Security. One international shipping company has a program that establishes strict physical and procedural security measures and requires thorough training throughout the corporation, from top management down to cover the entire workforce. This company has established standards for all contract carriers, subject those carriers to periodic audits to ensure standards compliance, and rely on strict contractual arrangements requiring 100% reimbursement in the event of a loss. When losses occur, the company requires the unit responsible for the loss to identify the exact cause of loss and propose methods to ensure that such a loss will not recur.

Planning

Develop an Emergency Plan. The Los Angeles County Metropolitan Transportation Authority (LACMTA) has developed a comprehensive emergency plan to establish the Incident Command System as the standard emergency operations system. The plan sets forth the policy and guidelines for the emergency procedures that are implemented by LACMTA and other responding agencies whenever a life-threatening situation occurs on or adjacent to the LACMTA system. Guidelines are provided for:

- Reporting the incident;
- Evaluation of the incident;
- Use of the incident command system;
- Notification of emergency response personnel/agencies;
- Protection of personnel and equipment at the incident site;
- Dispatch of emergency response personnel and equipment to the incident site;
- Evacuation of passengers;
- Use of rescue trains and other emergency vehicles;
- Keeping passengers, employees, emergency response personnel/agencies and others updated;
- Management of the emergency; and
- Restoring the system to normal.[33]

Develop a Long Range Policing Plan. The BART Police Department, in anticipation of the need for improved public transportation systems, has developed the Long Range BART District Policing Plan. The plan addresses future system concerns and how BART will shape this future by focusing on the safety and security of its district patrons, employees, and system property. BART's plan has been undertaken to determine the needs of transit districts and their patrons, and the most expeditious methods of meeting those needs. The issues and concerns that BART's plan addresses include the following:

- Environmental analysis;

---

[33] Roth, Kathryn A. *San Francisco Bay Area Rapid Transit District Emergency Plan,* 1994.

- Crime analysis and statistics;
- Major issues and concerns; and
- Reengineering and technological opportunities.

Chemical/Biological Incident Contingency Plan. In 1996, NYC's OEM established a committee to develop a Chemical/Biological Incident Contingency Plan. The Sarin gas attack in the Tokyo subway system and a no-notice test of New York's response to terrorist use of nerve gas in the subway system prompted officials to fast-track the contingency planning process. Five areas of special attention were identified:

- Coordination with the FBI;
- Being prepared for mass casualties;
- Treating incident as a crime scene;
- Need for speedy response actions to save lives; and
- Need for specialized training, equipment, and supplies.

Operation of Joint Terrorism Task Forces. The Federal Bureau of Investigation has created Joint Terrorism Task Forces (JTTF) to aid in the investigation of terrorism cases. The New York JTTF was created in 1976 and serves as the model for the country. The FBI employs state and federal local law enforcement officers under a Memorandum of Understanding and works side-by-side with the officers. The FBI also participated in the establishment of an International Terrorism Task Force that includes Secret Service agents, INS agents, ATF agents, and Customs agents. The JTTF and the ITTF allow for a coordinated and planned approach to the investigation of terrorist activity, as well as preparing for special events such as the Olympics, or the Republican and Democratic conventions.

Develop a System Security Program Plan. A recent FTA Rule for State Safety and Security Oversight (codified at 49 CFR Part 659) requires all rail transit systems to have prepared and implemented an SSPP by January 1, 1998. The SSPP must be based on planning guidelines contained in the FTA publications, *Transit System Security Program Planning Guide, Transit Security Procedures Guide,* and on the security planning requirements developed by the rail transit agency's State Safety Oversight Agency. The SSPP provides several important benefits, such as:

- The clear identification of all agency responsibilities for security and the education of all employees concerning those responsibilities;
- The opportunity to examine and strengthen key interfaces between the transit police/security department and the transit agency's operating and maintenance departments; and
- The opportunity to strengthen coordination and cooperation with local, state, and federal law enforcement and emergency services organizations.

The Greater Cleveland Regional Transit Authority has developed a system security program plan designed to adhere to FTA policy by maximizing security within the Cleveland RTA system by fully utilizing all available resources in the region in a coordinated manner.

Designate a Terrorism Preparedness Planning Group. Many transit police/security departments have designated planning groups within their departments to address terrorism. Planning groups may be pre-existing as part of corporate security structures or internal planning organizations designed to address ongoing security issues, or they may be created specifically to address terrorism. In some cases, inter-organizational committees have been used to take advantage of personnel expertise from throughout the transit agency.

Under the direction and influence of New York City's Office of Emergency Management, the Law Enforcement Focus Group was established, and includes representatives from federal, state, MTA, and neighboring state transportation authorities. The Law Enforcement Focus Group has developed plans and policies for interagency protocols to identify the following:

- Site security;
- Traffic control;
- Crime scene preservation and integrity;

- Identifying additional active devices; and
- First responder awareness.

Advance Planning for Special Events. In planning for special events, the Office of Intelligence and Security (S-60), operating within the Office of the Secretary of Transportation, works with the operating administrations of the U.S. Coast Guard (USCG); Federal Aviation Administration (FAA), Federal Railroad Administration (FRA); Federal Highway Administration (FHWA); Federal Transit Administration (FTA); Maritime Administration (MARAD), and the Research and Special Programs Administration (RSPA) to implement and coordinate security.

FRA. Although the FRA does not have regulatory authority to order rail carriers to reroute or limit rail activity during a special event, the FRA partnered with railroad carriers and Atlanta Olympics' organizers to develop an action plan to ensure the safe movement of rail traffic and reduction of hazardous material shipments by rail throughout the center city area of Atlanta during the games.

FHWA. Security measures for highways and bridges fall under state and local jurisdiction. Emergency Highway Traffic Regulation Plans are developed by each state to regulate traffic during emergency situations. When planning for a special event, specific issues are addressed:

- Traffic volume;
- Periods of congestion;
- Planned construction projects;
- Volume of hazardous materials transported;
- Plans for removal of abandoned vehicles which might conceal explosive devices; and
- Use of highways/streets for entrance or egress for terrorists.

Pipelines. Deliberate destruction of a pipeline carrying natural gas or petroleum products could cause severe injuries or property damage. Pipelines can, on occasion, run close to a special event site, and therefore must be taken into account when planning for the event.

Maritime. When reviewing maritime assets in planning for a special event, consideration must be given to vessels, passengers, cargoes, and the installations of the port facility itself, such as buildings, equipment, and follow-on transportation methods.

Transit. Most of the larger transit systems have in place a transit security plan which is administered either by a transit police force or an office of security which works in conjunction with local police. It is essential that these organizations maintain contact with event sponsors early in the planning stages for any special event.

The Utah Transit Authority has already begun to prepare for the year 2,000 Olympic Games in Salt Lake City. By anticipating possible events-related security issues, UTA may be able to diffuse situations that may arise. Their detailed security plan will:

- Secure ample personnel;
- Design and disseminate emergency procedures to help alleviate potentially serious situations;
- Coordinate transit security/police activities; and
- Coordinate with outside agencies (local police, events staff, city government).[34]

Require Passenger Terminal and Vessel Security Plans. Title 33 CFR parts 120 and 128, published on July 18, 1996 provides regulations for passenger vessel security for ships operating out of U.S. waters, over 100 gross tons, and carrying over 12 passengers on voyages over 24 hours to implement specific plans for ensuring passenger security. The regulation addresses both shipboard and terminal security measures that must be taken. It contains guidelines for incident reporting and descriptions of actions necessary at different threat levels (low, medium, and high). Key terminal elements include limiting unauthorized access to terminal areas, yearly security surveys, physical barriers, lighting, screening of passengers and baggage, designated restricted areas, and coordination with vessel operators. Vessel security plans must include designation of a security officer, yearly security surveys, standard operating procedures, alarms, lighting, communications, passenger and baggage screening, designation of restricted areas, and coordination with terminal operators.[35]

Response Planning. Control centers for rail operations, are in communication with specific authorities (local, state, and federal) to provide emergency response notification in the event of any major disaster, natural or manmade. Specific procedures exist for notification, control, and emergency response resources. Documentation at the location is typically identified as the Emergency Response Plan (ERP) and has become part of the operating procedures. The ERPs are regionally designated for the operating district on the railroads.

Coordination

Coordination of efforts must begin before an actual disaster strikes. Emergency agencies should work together to establish effective channels of communication and to standardize procedures in emergency response efforts. Three levels of response often categorize transit emergencies:

- Single jurisdiction responsibility with single agency involvement;
- Single jurisdiction responsibility with multi-agency involvement; and
- Multi-jurisdiction responsibility with multi-agency involvement.

Transit agencies must be prepared to coordinate with external agencies for each of these response levels.[36]

---

[34] Boyd, Maier & Associates, Inc. "Addressing Events-Related Violence," *Transit Policing,* Vol. 5 n. 1, Fall 1995.

[35] U.S. Coast Guard Navigation and Vessel Inspection Circular No. 3-96

[36] Boyd, Maier & Associates, Inc. 1997. *Critical Incident Management Guidelines,* p. 4-4.

Coordination with Local, State, and Federal Agencies. A key element in any terrorism planning program is the access to intelligence on potential terrorist threats and activities. In the event of an actual incident, effective multi-agency coordination is essential. To meet these requirements, transit police departments and transit agencies have developed and are enhancing programs to maximize communication and coordination with local, state, and federal agencies.

Many transit agencies are actively involved with state and city emergency organizations, and participate in meetings, committees, councils, and planning groups. In addition, local and transit police officials maintain contact with other municipal and federal law enforcement agencies in the course of regular crime prevention activities. Additional interaction occurs through joint investigations and joint planning efforts for special events, and through interagency groups, such as professional law enforcement associations that meet to discuss crime-related issues.

Understanding jurisdictional relationships is a key component of effective coordination. Response to a terrorist incident is likely to be emotionally charged and highly confusing. When jurisdictional roles have been resolved, either in a MOU or a similar document, individual agency responsibilities will be easier to identify. Such an understanding supports the capabilities of both the transit agency and its local response organizations to provide advance information on possible terrorist activity, as well as cross training, and joint-preparation programs and operations.[37]

Agreements with Other Transit Agencies. Transit agencies can provide voluntary assistance to each other to ensure that public transportation services continue throughout the region to the maximum extent practical during major service interruptions. Assistance is generally in the form of equipment, supplies, and personnel. Transit agencies in the San Francisco area have formed the San Francisco Bay Area Transit Operators Agreement. The participants are:

- Alameda-Contra Costa Transit District;
- San Francisco BART District;
- Contra Costa County Transportation Authority;
- Golden Gate Bridge, Highway, and Transportation District;
- Livermore-Amador Valley Transit Authority;
- San Francisco Municipal Railway (MUNI);
- San Mateo County Transit District;
- Santa Clara County Transit District; and
- City of Vallejo.

Inter-organizational Emergency Memoranda of Understanding (MOU). Inter-organizational Memoranda of Understanding serve as the basis of mutual acknowledgement of the resources that each organization will provide during response and recovery efforts. Transit agencies developing inter-organizational emergency MOUs, may include the following elements:

- A list of participating emergency response organization;
- Definition of jurisdictional boundaries for primary responding organizations;
- Detailed definition of the chain of command, and of control, communication, and evacuation procedures;
- Statement of how proposed changes to procedures will be reviewed and approved;
- Description of and instructions for operation of specialized emergency equipment;
- Description of transit system personnel and their duties; and
- Training responsibilities.[38]

---

[37] Boyd, Annabelle and Sullivan, John P., 1997. "Emergency Preparedness for Transit Terrorism," *Synthesis of Transit Practice 27*, National Academy Press, Washington D.C., pp. 18-19.

[38] Boyd, Maier & Associates, Inc. 1997. *Critical Incident Management Guidelines*, p. 4-5.

Rail Police. Physical security of railroads in the U.S. is supplied by in-house police forces, comprised of a total of about 2,800 officers. These officers are commissioned in the state of their primary employment and are trained and licensed in the same manner as other state-certified police officers. Railroad police have arrest authority in all states in which the employing railroad owns property. Railroad police maintain a working relationship with local law enforcement agencies as well as national and international authorities such as the FBI, DEA, and INTERPOL.

Amtrak Police. Amtrak has a police force of 346 officers to protect passengers, employees and physical assets of the system. Over 80% of these forces are assigned to the intensely populated and high service line between Washington, D.C. and Boston. This method of deployment averages out to 1 security person for every 55 miles of track.

Track Inspection. All railroads, including Amtrak, are required to perform periodic physical track inspections. All mainline and sidings with over 10 MGT per year must be inspected a minimum of twice within a given seven-day period, with at least one day between inspections. In addition, railroads depend on track condition monitoring via "trip reports" completed and submitted by locomotive engineers to note and identify potential hazardous conditions.

- Assignment Checklists
- Resources Plan
- Communications Plan
- Medical Plan
- Facilities Traffic Plan.
- Safety Plan
- Demobilization Plan

Development of Incident Management Tools

Develop an Incident Action Plan. The Law Enforcement Branch of the Governor's Office of Emergency Services in California has developed the Law Enforcement Guide of Emergency Operations, which includes a comprehensive Incident Action Plan (IAP). The IAP follows emergency service guidelines and includes the following planning areas:

- Overall Objectives & Priorities
- Incident Objectives
- Organization Chart
- Assignment Checklists
- Resources Plan
- Communications Plan
- Medical Plan
- Safety Plan
- Demobilization Plan

Develop an Emergency Response Structure. Emergency Action Plans that are heavily influenced by the Incident Command System (ICS) provide the required flexibility to rapidly establish and activate an organizational structure around emergency requirements. Using designated functional sections, agencies have the flexibility to develop the form of the responding organization to match required tasks and the ability to staff only those functional sections that are necessary to resolve the incident.

Perhaps the most important feature of the ICS is its ability to be integrated into the command structure of local police and fire departments. In the event of an actual terrorist incident at a transit system, either local police or fire services ultimately assume the duties of the incident commander, or join in a "unified command."

Bus Mobile Command. New Jersey Transit mechanics and maintenance personnel converted a bus into a mobile command post complete with restroom, whiteboards, and incident management forms and checklists. This allowed NJT to mobilize its critical incident management response structure, thus adding flexibility to the command functions needed at the necessary field location.

Incident Response Checklist Kits. A growing emergency response procedure industry wide, is the use of pre-printed Incident Response Forms that outline response guidelines. Kept in mobile response unit, police automobiles as well, first responders use the checklists to guide them through first responder activities.

ITS Ability to Support Emergency Response. ITS systems are being employed in some cities to help direct emergency vehicles, such as ambulances, fire trucks, and police cars, to respond quickly. The same systems could provide emergency response capabilities for situations such as terrorist activities where a large-scale response must be coordinated.

Training and Drills

Crisis Intervention Training. The Long Island Railroad police staff has researched and developed the *Crisis Intervention/Management within Confined Spaces* program, designed to assist and guide transit personnel in at-risk situations. The course enables them to:

- Identify potential crisis situations;
- Prevent incidents or events from escalating into a full crisis;
- Diffuse the situation as much as possible by use of communication skills;
- Isolate the person(s);
- Stabilize the situation;
- Communicate essential and accurate information regarding an ongoing situation to control tower operators, central dispatcher and responding police officers;
- Maintain the stabilized situation until the arrival of properly trained law enforcement and emergency response personnel; and
- Understand the stressful effect of crisis situations on passengers and transit crew, and the value of procedures for appropriate stress reduction counseling.[39]

Deployment Techniques. Many transit agencies use different methods of security/police personnel deployment in an effort to either prevent terrorist activity, or to reduce the impact of terrorism. Deployment techniques such as

police patrol and surveillance and coordination with operations and maintenance personnel aid in the identification and resolution of security threats. In light of a new and expanded focus to include defense against terrorism, the Long Island Rail Road (LIRR) Police Department trains officers and the employees of LIRR in such aspects of terrorism prevention such as how to search for suspicious packages and how to evacuate impacted areas.

Emergency Medical Rescue Units. New York City Transit Police has employed officers, some of which are registered nurses, emergency medical technicians, or certified in advanced first aid, who volunteer their time to the Transit Police Emergency Medical Rescue Unit (EMRU). The sixty transit police officers that make up the EMRU are well trained in emergency response, thus strengthening NYCT's preparedness in the event of an emergency or critical incident.[40]

Conduct Interagency Drills. The Office of System Safety within the Metropolitan Transportation Authority-New York City Transit conducts four Interagency Emergency Preparedness Drills per year as part of a continuous effort to promote emergency responder familiarity with the unique transit environment as well as to foster interagency coordination during real emergencies on NYCT property. Outside agencies that are primary participants include:

- New York City Fire Department (FDNY);
- New York City Police Department (NYPD); and
- Emergency Medical Services (EMS).

Support functions are provided by:

- New York City of Department of Environmental Protection (DEP)
- New York City Department of Traffic (DOT)
- Mayor's Office of Emergency Management (OEM)

---

[39] Obremski, Frank L. and Wendel, Charles. "Crisis Intervention for Mass Transit Systems," *Transit Policing,* Vol. 4 n. 2, Fall 1994.

[40] Albert O'Leary. "Super Cops of the Subway," *Transit Policing* Vol. 3 n. 1, Winter/Spring 1993.

- Salvation Army of Greater New York
- American Red Cross[41]

Safety Training. Wisconsin Central Railroad (WCR) and the Federal Railroad Administration have renewed the voluntary safety compliance agreement they reached in 1997. Under the new agreement, WCR will continue to take specific steps to improve track and equipment inspection, training measures, and operating practices. The agreement "goes beyond existing federal regulations to ensure the next level of rail safety throughout the Wisconsin Central Railroad network," said FRA Administrator Jolene Molitoris.

The original agreement was signed in February 1997. As part of the agreement, WCR has agreed to suspend most operations with one-person train crews, and to refrain from remote control
operations, except when confined to industrial plants.[42]

Response

During the ***Response Phase***, the transportation operator must resolve the occurrence of a single critical incident. These activities ensure the development of comprehensive operations plans for coordinating multi-agency response to the critical incident. This response is guided by cooperatively-established incident objectives which ensure the efficient resolution of the incident and the safety of both affected persons and property and transportation and public safety response personnel:

- First response;
- Implementing ICS/UCS;
- Incident management; and
- Crisis communications.

The best practices identified for this phase of emergency management range from the highly technical nature of SCADA system management

to the more traditional Incident Command System implementation. Training and contingency planning provide the different modes of transport with guidelines for addressing emergency response efforts. Railway agreements allow for the cooperation between different railroads for the diverting of trains when required due to an emergency or critical incident. In the transit industry, very detailed emergency plans outline the steps necessary for emergency response. The NYCT Police developed the First Responder Checklist to guide first responder actions in emergency situations.

In addition to incident management structures and protocols, necessary for a successful response to an incident, many agencies have developed communication procedures to follow, in order to maintain constant contact between the responders at the scene, and central authorities.

Key incident objectives for managing response to transit terrorism can be categorized into *general responses* and *transit-specific responses*.

Objectives for general response to terrorist incidents.

- Secure perimeters (establish inner and outer perimeters and control zones; contain the situation; avoid creating new victims, contaminating evidence, and spreading contaminants).
- Control and identify the threat (including CBN agent release).
- Rescue, decontaminate, triage, treat, and transport impacted persons.
- Move crowds to safe zones (minimize additional casualties).
- Stabilize incident (prevent escalation, establish control of the situation to allow rescue and recovery to proceed with minimal delay).
- Protect rescuers (injured responders cannot effectively rescue and place an additional strain on scarce resources, potentially jeopardizing operational success). All response personnel should receive an incident specific safety briefing

---

[41] Norman Y. Mineta International Institute for Surface Transportation Policy Studies, 1991. *Terrorism in Surface Transportation,* San Jose State University. Appendix A.
[42] Train It! Volume V, Number 3, 2/19/98.

when extraordinary hazards exist. All personnel should be provided and required to wear and use Personal Protective Equipment (PPE) appropriate to incident conditions.

- Avoid secondary contamination.
- Secure evidence and crime scene (evidence management and crime scene issues are important to the identification of offenders and future prosecution; inner and outer perimeters and proper procedures must be followed).
- Protect against secondary attack (global experience with terrorist attacks and bombings has shown that secondary attack, [i.e., secondary explosive devices intended to injure emergency responders], is a real threat).

Objectives for transit-specific concerns.

- Provide alternative modes of transport.
- Assess and mitigate secondary impact on system (crowd conditions throughout the system, particularly at key transfer points, are likely depending on the site of the incident; additionally, agencies should maintain a high index of suspicion for additional attacks or "copycat" incidents in the immediate aftermath of an attack).
- Restore service quickly (restore transit service through re-routed vehicles and alternative modes, [i.e., "bus bridges"]. Clearing the incident scene and repairing damaged areas must be a priority).
- Restore passenger confidence (on-going security measures must be reinforced. Transit customers should be advised of enhanced awareness and measures).
- Restore employee confidence (integrate employees into system security team).

First Response

When a terrorist incident or disaster occurs, a large number of people and agencies will be called upon to address the many individual actions required to resolve the incident. This process will be initiated by the first responders

from a number of disciplines. At a rail transit system, such responders may include the transit police, transit operations personnel, local police, and the fire and emergency medical services. During this immediate response phase, efforts will be focused on assessment of the situation (also known as "size-up") to develop a situation estimate, containment of the incident (through police lines, fire lines, or a perimeter) to prevent additional casualties and preserve evidence, the search for additional terrorist devices, and notifications.

Essentially, first responders need to establish on-scene command, develop a situation estimate, request necessary personnel and equipment for the scene, and establish a command post and staging (and mobilization) area to receive and effectively deploy in-coming personnel and equipment. In a terrorist incident, on-scene command usually will be initiated by the police (either transit or local law enforcement) with the intention to develop a "unified command" among key response agencies (i.e., police, fire, emergency medical, and in latter stages investigative personnel from the Federal Bureau of Investigation, the National Transportation Safety Board, etc.).

The situation estimate developed from the initial assessment should contain the following information:

- Type of emergency;
- Location;
- Size of involved area;
- The number and type of casualties;
- Special hazards; and
- Assistance required (i.e., number of police officers, transit vehicles, utilities, etc.).

Operation Respond. Operation Respond is a non-profit institution designed to improve the information available to first responders at hazardous material or passenger rail accident sites. Operation Respond provides emergency response personnel with on-site training in dealing with passenger train emergency situations. It is also developing a software system that provides immediate online information to rescue personnel as to the location and operation of emergency exits and systems in passenger cars.

CSXT Donates a Communication System to a West Virginia Rescue Squad. CSXT donated the Operation Respond Emergency Information System (OREIS), a communications system developed by Operation Respond, to the Huntington-Cabell County 911 Center in Huntington, W.Va. OREIS will link the county dispatch center to the databases of participating rail and motor carriers that operate in West Virginia to enable emergency responders to react quickly and effectively during a hazardous materials incident. Among the information available to emergency response teams is the type of hazardous material being carried, its characteristics and information that allows the emergency team to respond and react to the incident in a safe manner, for themselves and the communities they serve.[43]

Use of SCADA Systems to Monitor Pipelines. Many companies use SCADA Software applications packages that provide the capability to detect and locate leaks and track batches of products in the pipeline. A SCADA system monitors flow rates, pressures, and temperatures at various locations such as well-heads, valves on the pipeline, and pump stations. SCADA systems are also used to track inventory of products delivered to storage tanks, refineries, custody transfer points or to the consumer.

Most companies use two host computers for the SCADA System, with one acting as a backup. In the event of the failure of the primary host computer, the backup takes over. Several of the major SCADA systems have complete back-up systems located in different cities and on different power and communications grids. The master control station hosts the SCADA software, database, and applications software. Graphic workstations are connected to the master station computers providing the Man-Machine Interface for operators to monitor and

control operations of the system. Front-end computers link the communications channels to the master station and poll the remote devices for data. The master station computers periodically poll the front-end computers to update the master database from which status information is relayed to the operator's console.

Systems often use a mix of communication mediums for the remote monitoring and control devices so that the loss of one medium does not render the system inoperable. An important function within the SCADA system is the management of the remote communications circuits of the system. The communications network is the backbone of the SCADA system. Connectivity to remote monitoring and control devices is typically provided by dedicated copper, fiber-optic circuits, wireless communications (RF/microwave), and telecommunications circuits using leased lines and commercial telephone service.

Most companies have a certain level of local control at pumping or compressor stations, terminals, etc. This allows the pipeline to continue operation without the SCADA system (typically at reduced capacity) by manning the local control stations with local operators. In these situations, the pipeline operators issue control commands to the local operators via radio or telephone.

Implementing ICS/UCS

ICS Integration. The Incident Command System is the basis for standard operating policies and procedures or the mobilization of BART and other public safety resources. In BART's Emergency Plan, the ICS is used to manage emergencies and allows agencies to communicate using common terminology and operating procedures. In addition to the standardized terminology, BART's Incident Command System provides for the following:

- Modular organization;
- Integrated communications;
- Unified command structure;
- Consolidate action plans;
- Manageable span of control;

---

[43] Train It! Volume IV, Number 24, 12/19/97.

- Designated incident facilities; and
- Comprehensive resource management.

Activating the ICS. For most agencies, whether they are public safety organizations or transit operations, a key element of first response is activating the ICS. For police and fire departments, the first responder to the scene generally becomes the Incident Commander. At LIRR, the first police officer to arrive at a crime scene takes charge to protect and collect evidence. The first fire department officer to arrive at a LIRR emergency scene is in charge until the fire is out. Command is transferred to a higher-ranking officer at such a time as is appropriate during the response effort.[44]

Incident Management

Critical Incident Management Checklist. The New York City Transit (NYCT) Police developed a First Responder Checklist to guide first responder actions at all critical incidents. Such a checklist provides an easy method for focusing first response activities. NYCT identified the following critical tasks:

- Assess nature of incident
  - Exact location
  - Extent of casualties and carnage
  - Most limiting factors (what must be done to bring it under control)
  - Whether there are sufficient resources on the scene
  - Assistance required
  - Probable effect of incident on other areas

- Communicate results of assessment to:
  - Communication unit
  - Relieving supervisor

- Provide direction to responding units (from street to staging area)

- Establish perimeters
  - Inner perimeter (to prevent further injury at location of problem)

- Outer perimeter (to retain control of area used by responding units for command posts and staging areas)

- Provide rescue and first aid

- Identify and control access routes
  - From scene to local hospital(s)
  - Form local commands to scene
  - At the scene (vehicle parking)

- Incident priorities (police objectives)
  - Protect life and provide safety
  - Prevent further injury or damage
  - Protect property
  - Restore order

Critical Incident Management Guide. In addition to the checklist above, the New York City Transit Police have also developed a Critical Incident Management Guide to assist in the training of those personnel who might one day respond to an emergency. The guidelines address common errors in critical incident management, as well as outline the following:

- Incident response objectives;
  - Management concepts;
  - Organization;
  - Communication strategies; and
  - Incident command structure.

The guide also acts as a tool to establish a foundation on which an interagency training program can be based.

Railway Agreements/Cooperation. Both formal and informal agreements between railroads provide for track usage by diverted trains where and when required, typically in natural disaster scenarios. A good example of this kind of cooperation, Burlington Northern Santa Fe and Union Pacific have begun operating a joint regional dispatching center for Gulf Coast train operations in Spring, a Houston suburb.

The center will control train operations between Houston and New Orleans over more than 340 miles of track to be jointly owned by both railroads, as well as main line trackage formerly operated by the Houston Belt & Terminal

---

[44] Boyd, Maier & Associates, Inc. 1997. *Critical Incident Management Guidelines*, p. 6-6.

Railroad and a portion of the Port Terminal Railroad Association in Houston. The center is designed to improve coordination of train operations and communication among all the railroads serving the Houston area, as well as improve the efficiency of yards serving the area.[45]

Crisis Communications

Maintain Communication Capabilities. Communications is one of the most important considerations in any successful response to a critical incident, whether caused by intentional or unintentional acts. When responding to an emergency, centralized and systematized communication must be maintained. BART's Fire Department has included methods by which the Incident Commander can maintain a line of communication with BART Central, as well as within the BART System, in their emergency manual. BART's communication considerations include:

- Maintenance Telephones. Provides numerous telephone access points for maintenance personnel to communicate with BART Central.

- PABX Phone System. The Private Automatic Branch System provides two way direct dial telephone communication links among BART personnel.

- Emergency Telephone. BART's Blue Line Phone emergency system is for making direct calls to BART Central from the Transbay Tube, subways, and tunnels. Simply lifting the handset places the caller in an immediate connection with an operator.

- Mine Phone System. This system allows for people to signal or alert others in the Transbay Tube lower gallery. When the page button is pressed, communications

are heard over the speakers at all other phone locations.

- Command Post Telephones. This system consists of a Yellow Phone (dedicated firefighter phone), Black Phone (an extension dial pone line on Oakland and San Francisco Fire Departments telephone systems), Green Phone (private lines between Fire Department Command Posts), and Red Phone (provide direct circuit link between Fire Department Command Posts and extend to BART Central Control).

- Radios. Provide two-way communication between mobile units and BART Central.

- BART Fire Channel. Used by Berkeley, Oakland, Orinda, and San Francisco Fire Departments for underground firefighting communications.

- Station Public Address Systems.

In addition to the standard communication operation procedures, BART's Emergency Plan provides an Emergency Information Flow Chart. For each emergency, the flow chart outlines the process for emergency information dissemination.

Since the Sunset Limited Incident, Amtrak has Begun to Maintain Regular and Closer Contact With Law Enforcement and Rescue Services. Towards that end, Amtrak police have placed greater emphasis on maintaining closer links with the National Association of Sheriffs and the National Association of Police Chiefs.

Recovery

During the *Recovery Phase*, transportation operators and public safety organizations clear the emergency scene, conduct investigations, and restore service. These activities result in recovery plans, which ensure the appropriate staging and operation of essential equipment and vehicles and the implementation of inter-organizational agreements with other

---

[45] Train It! Volume V, Number 5, 3/19/98.

transportation providers (for re-routing and scheduling):

- Demobilization and Redeployment
- Incident Debriefing and After Action Reports
- Clean-up and Service Restoration
- Critical Incident Stress Management
- Restoring Confidence.

Restoring service involves shifting incident management efforts from the response phase to the recovery phase. The focus moves from activities such as the rescue of injured persons, evacuations to prevent additional injuries and firefighting to preparing trains, rights-of-way, stations and facilities to once again moving passengers. This shift, however, does not occur solely at the command of incident management personnel on the scene or monitoring operations from a control center or EOC. Rather, recovery must begin *during* the response phase to ensure an effective return to normal operations.

In major incidents, recovery may require replacing track and ballast, building temporary stations, and obtaining new equipment. Such efforts can be accomplished in less time if mechanisms for obtaining materials and personnel for system reconstruction are identified in advance.

Demobilization and Redeployment

Demobilization Plan. A major incident results in the mobilization of personnel from a number of agencies and disciplines. After the initial stabilization on the incident scene, some responders may complete their respective missions and be replaced by others who will assume new ones. California's Law Enforcement Guide of Emergency Operations outlines the specific procedures for demobilization of incident personnel. The Demobilization Unit assigned to planning intelligence prepares the Demobilization Plan.

Incident Debriefing and After Action Reports

Incident Debriefing and After Action Reports. The response to every significant accident or disruption of service should also be evaluated to identify strengths and deficiencies. All personnel who participate in the response should be debriefed after responding to each emergency.

WMATA, in recognition that every complex incident is different in terms of behavior, staffing, and mobilization, uses Incident Debriefing and After Action Reports extensively as a way to:

- Review interagency relationships and minimize interagency misunderstandings;
- Review decision-making processes;
- Ensure a formal review of problems encountered; and
- Learn from innovations developed during incidents.

Clean-up and Service Restoration

Once response activities are concluded, the incident scene can be cleaned up and preparations for restoring normal operations can begin. Some incidents, for example those involving hazardous materials, require outside contractors to remove environmental contaminants. In all cases, the incident scene will have to be assessed. Automated equipment must be tested by safety engineers to ensure its capability to safely resume operations. Finally, all response and recovery personnel must be advised when service resumes. Response and recovery personnel must also replenish supplies to ensure readiness in case of new incidents.

Automated Resource Inventory. New Jersey Transit (NJT) uses an Automated Resource Inventory as a tool to ensure that the clean-up and restoration process is as efficient as possible. This inventory resource system allows NJT to search different localities with the district, public and private, to find that equipment that is necessary for the clean-up process. In the aftermath of a recent commuter rail incident, NJT was able to clear tracks and restore service due in large part to the use of crane equipment located at a nearby construction site through the automated resource inventory system.

Use of Contractors for Clean-up. Since those responsible for maintenance of the transportation network may not have access to the expertise needed to clean up after an intentional act or unintentional event involving a hazardous material, some localities rely on contracted assistance that can be utilized should a need arise.

Critical Incident Stress Management

Stress Management Planning. Facing widespread devastation challenges even the most resolute and experienced emergency responder. Recognition of the long-term effects of critical incident stress has led to the development, by many agencies, of Critical Incident Stress Debriefing. The Long Island Rail Road Police Department has developed the Crisis Intervention/Management Training Program (CIMTP) to give transit crews and operating personnel recommended guidelines for identifying and handling persons who appear to be at risk of, or who are already experiencing a crisis. The CIMTP was developed to be a multi-phase approach addressing the following techniques:

- Indicators of Emotional Disturbances;
- Causes of Emotional Disturbances;
- Low-High Risk Situations;
- Risk Assessment;
- Handling Crisis Situations; and
- Stress Debriefing.

Restoring Confidence

One of the goals of terrorism is to strike terror into the hearts of the public and erode its confidence. In the aftermath of a transit terrorist incident, passenger and employee confidence must be restored. After the 1995 bombing campaign against Paris transit systems, ridership declined. In Israel, warnings of terrorist bombings against buses in October 1996 resulted in a 20 percent drop in intracity bus travel according to Israeli officials. Immediate, positive actions by the transit system and police are vital in restoring confidence and countering fear.

In the aftermath of the Paris bombings, French police adopted high profile patrols. The system broadcast announcements asking passengers to be alert and to report any suspicious packages, and transit personnel distributed handouts urging passengers to be vigilant. Eight thousand trashcans were sealed the day after the December 4, 1996 bombing.

Similar steps have been adopted in the aftermath of other notable events. Police at several systems heightened uniformed patrols on trains and at terminals immediately after the Long Island Rail Road shooting and the Fulton Street Firebombing. In several cases, these patrols were publicized in the local media. Steps to bolster employee confidence have included security and bomb awareness briefings conducted by transit police for transit personnel and the following publicity campaigns:

- Radio advertisements;
- Flyers;
- Saturation patrol; and
- Engage and reassure public.

After the bomb exploded in Centennial Park during the 1996 Olympics in Atlanta, MARTA officials made a conscientious effort to keep the public informed of changes to its service, entry and exit points, and station facilities. The bombing incident ended up having little or no effect upon the public's confidence in MARTA.

APPENDIX B – ITS SECURITY REQUIREMENTS

General ITS Security Requirements

It should be noted that a few general security requirements apply to all ITS systems. These requirements are administrative in nature and will be presented first followed by technical security requirements for the Center, Roadside, Vehicle, and Remote Access systems.

Recommended Security Requirements

- Devices utilized to provide ITS security must be based on open standards, conform to appropriate security standards where such standards exist, communicate utilizing international or U.S. standards-based protocols, and employ commercial off-the-shelf (COTS) technology that has been subjected to due diligence whenever possible.
- A formal, role-based access approval procedure for individual users should be implemented and enforced for each Center system and Center System data processing facility and should be used to adhere to a principle of"least privilege."
- All custom software applications should successfully pass formal test procedures prior to installation in ITS.
- ITS security requirements should be incorporated into planning for and the design of all new ITS and any invitation for bids or other solicitation for ITS or ITS components should include security as a weighted evaluation factor.
- Configuration management must be exercised on all ITS software and hardware systems.
- An ITS Security Officer should be

appointed to ensure compliance with established ITS security standards and perform internal system audits. Further, consideration should be given to the establishment of an ITS Security Working Group.
- A formal contingency/disaster recovery plan and procedures must be established for each ITS system and contingency/disaster recovery procedures should be tested on a periodic basis.
- ITS operational data should be backed up as appropriate to its criticality and a copy stored off site consistent with contingency/disaster recovery plan procedures.
- An information processing security training and awareness program must be implemented for ITS.

Center Systems

Center subsystems are the "heart" of the ITS architecture. It is these systems which deal with all those functions normally assigned to public/private administrative, management, or planning agencies. ITS Centers consist of the following subsystems:

- Traffic Management
- Emissions Management
- Transit Management
- Toll Administration
- Commercial Vehicle Administration
- Information Service Provider
- Emergency Management
- Freight and Fleet Management
- Planning

Recommended Security Requirements

- Center System application, communication, data, and file servers *(servers)* should implement a role-based identification and authentication policy and mechanism sufficiently robust to protect system criticality.
- Center System role-based access control mechanisms should be used to enforce a *least privilege* security policy.
- Each user of Center System *servers* should be assigned a unique identifier to support *least privilege* access control processing.
- Each user of Center System *servers* should be assigned a unique personal authentication code, such as a password, to authenticate his/her unique identifier.
- Each Center System *server* should implement an audit function appropriate to the criticality of the system.
- Center System *server* remote access controllers should incorporate mechanisms to defeat masquerade of an authorized user by malicious attack.
- Direct access to Center System *servers* from Intranets, Extranets, and the Internet should be inhibited.
- An appropriate mechanism should be implemented to continuously validate the integrity of data entering a Central System.
- An appropriate mechanism should be implemented to continuously authenticate the source of data entering a Central System.
- A mechanism should be implemented to ensure non-repudiation of appropriate data entering a Central System.
- A mechanism should be implemented for Central System *servers* to guarantee the integrity and authenticity of data they provide to other systems.
- A mechanism to uniquely identify individuals authorized unrestricted access to Center System data processing facilities should be implemented.
- Communications between Center

Systems that transfer credit card, personal identification number (PIN), and/or other sensitive information to other ITS and terminator subsystems should utilize pair-wise encryption.

Roadside Systems

Roadside Systems are essential to the support of critical ITI functions. Traffic signal control, freeway management, electronic fare payment, electronic toll collection, and commercial vehicle operations are all supported by these systems.

Roadway Subsystem (RS). The RS includes the equipment distributed on and along the roadway, which monitors and controls traffic. Equipment includes highway advisory radios, variable message signs, closed circuit television (CCTV) cameras, and video image processing systems for incident detection and verification, vehicle detectors, traffic signal, and grade crossing warning systems. The subsystem also provides the capability for emissions monitoring in tunnels, and environmental condition monitoring including weather sensors and pavement icing sensors.

Commercial Vehicle Check Subsystem (CVCS). The CVCS is necessary to the support of commercial vehicle operations. Although commercial vehicle operations are not currently considered an essential element of the ITI in the national architecture, it is of growing in some states such as Maryland. Maryland is at the forefront of this technology which provides for automated checks and inspections of commercial vehicles at roadside, frequently while the vehicles remain in motion. The systems within the vehicles themselves are not the responsibility of the state but the state is responsible for CVCS systems that interface with the commercial vehicle and with the center subsystems that manage this activity. Collectively, these systems are known as the

CVISN project. Connectivity between the roadside and center subsystems is provided exclusively by wireline communications while two-way, short-range wireless communications is used between the commercial vehicles and roadside systems.

Parking Management Subsystem (PMS).
The PMS supports cash and electronic payments via credit card and will support payment by vehicle transponders.

Toll Collection Subsystem (TCS).
A TCS supports the toll collection infrastructure within the State. This infrastructure includes highways, bridges, and tunnels that are an important source of State revenue. The TCS interacts with vehicles to collect tolls and identify violators. Communications between the TCS and the central toll administration system is via wireline while communications with vehicle systems is via two-way, short-range wireless communications.

Recommended Security Requirements

- Communications between critical Roadside Systems and their respective Center System and other ITS and terminator subsystems should incorporate a sensor data integrity mechanism.
- Communications between critical Roadside Systems and their respective Center System and other ITS and terminator subsystems should incorporate a sensor data authentication mechanism.
- Communications between Roadside Systems that transfer credit card, personal identification number (PIN), and/or other sensitive information to their respective Center System and other ITS and terminator subsystems should utilize pair-wise encryption.
- Communications between critical Roadside Systems and their respective Center System and other ITS and terminator subsystems should incorporate a data authentication mechanism.

- Roadside System devices should include a mechanism to verify the integrity and authenticity of commands, program, and configuration data received.
- Roadside System devices should include a mechanism to support identification and authentication of personnel utilizing the device craft/maintenance port.

Vehicle Systems

Vehicle Systems are essential to the support of critical ITI functions. Emergency notification, transit vehicle operations, and electronic payment of parking fees and tolls are all supported by these systems.

Commercial Vehicle Subsystem (CVS).
The CVS is being developed by the private sector. Interfaces between the CVS and government supported CVCS are addressed in the security requirements for the CVCS.

Emergency Vehicle Subsystem (EVS).
The EVS is being developed by the private sector. No current or future interfaces between the EVS and government supported subsystems have been identified to date.

Transit Vehicle Subsystem (TRVS).
The TRVS is installed on public mass transit vehicles. The TRVS communicates with the onboard sensors via wireline, with the Roadside System via 2-way short-range wireless, and with Central Systems via 2-way wide area wireless telecommunications links.

The security concerns for the TRVS include availability. Most of the TRVS ITS functions **cannot** be performed in the absence of the two-way wide area wireless network. If the communications network is down, travelers will be inconvenienced, but public safety will not be jeopardized.

Vehicle Subsystem (VS).
A critical VS is the onboard transponder which is used for electronic payment of parking fees and tolls. These devices are developed by the private

sector. They normally take the form of small stickers that are typically installed on vehicle windshields.

Recommended Security Requirements

- Vehicle System identification tokens (e.g., bar code tags) should include an anti-tamper mechanism to foil theft.
- Vehicle System identification tokens (e.g., bar code tags) should include an authentication mechanism.
- Vehicle System identification tokens (e.g., bar code tags) should include a non-repudiation mechanism.
- Vehicle System identification tokens (e.g., bar code tags) should include an integrity mechanism.
- Vehicle Systems that transfer credit card, personal identification number (PIN), and/or other sensitive information should utilize pair-wise encryption.
- Vehicle System transponder communications should incorporate a transponder data integrity mechanism.
- Vehicle System data communications should incorporate a data integrity mechanism.
- Critical Vehicle System transponder communications should incorporate a transponder data authentication mechanism.
- Critical Vehicle System data communications should incorporate a data authentication mechanism.
- Critical Vehicle System should include a mechanism to verify the integrity and authenticity of commands, program, and configuration data received.
- Vehicle System devices should include a mechanism to support identification and authentication of personnel utilizing the device craft/maintenance port.

Remote Access Systems

Remote Access Systems are essential to the support of critical ITI functions. Emergency notification and acknowledgment are supported by these systems.

Personal Information Access Subsystem (PIAS). PIAS platforms such as the hand-held personal digital assistant (PDA) are developed by the private sector for use in applications like traveler information dissemination. Some state models have established traveler information bulletin boards in cyberspace and support read-only access by the public to this information. The public can access information via the Internet.

Regardless of the specific forms of interfaces made available to the public, safeguards must be in place to deny the availability of any and all protected resources, including data bases, to PIAS users.

Remote Traveler Support Subsystem (RTS). Kiosks are being deployed and interfaced with the Operations Centers through leased and auto dial lines. Safeguards must be in place to deny the availability of any and all protected resources, including data bases, to Kiosk users.

Recommended Security Requirements

- Remote Access Systems that transfer credit card, personal identification number (PIN), and/or other sensitive information should utilize pair-wise encryption.
- Remote Access Systems should include a traveler identification and authentication mechanism for sensitive transactions.
- Remote Access Systems should include a non-repudiation mechanism for sensitive transactions.
- Remote Access Systems transactions should include a data authentication mechanism.

APPENDIX C - ACRONYMS

ACES	- Automated Cargo Expediting System
ADPA	- American Defense Preparedness Association
AEI	- Automated Equipment Identification
ANFO	- Ammonium Nitrate Fuel Oil
ASAC	- Aviation Security Advisor Committee
ASIS	- American Society for Industrial Security
ATA	- American Trucking Association, Inc.
ATAA	- Air Transport Association of America
AVL	- Automatic Vehicle Location
BART	- Bay Area Rapid Transit District
BATF	- Bureau of Alcohol, Tobacco and Firearms
BDA	- Battle Damage Assessments
BW	- Biological Weapons
CAB	- Civil Aeronautics Board
CATS	- Consequences Assessment Tool Kit
C/B	- Chemical and Biological
CBN	- Chemical, Biological and Nuclear
CBW	- Chemical and Biological Weapons
CDC	- Centers for Disease Control
CFR	- Code of Federal Regulation
CNN	- Cable News Network
COFC	- Container-On- Flat-Car
COTP	- Captain Of The Port
CTA	- Chicago Transit Authority
CVISN	- Commercial Vehicle Information Systems and Network
CW	- Chemical Warfare
DART	- Dallas Area Rapid Transit Authority
DCS	- Distributed Control System
DEA	- Drug Enforcement Administration

DOD   - Department of Defense

DOE   - Department of Energy, United States

DOT   - Department of Transportation United States

DST   - Double-Stack-Train

EDI   - Electric Data Interchange

EMA   - Emergency Management Agency

EMS   - Emergency Medical Services

FAA   - Federal Aviation Administration, DOT

FBI   - Federal Bureau Investigation

FEMA   - Federal Emergency Management Agency

FHWA   - Federal Highway Administration, DOT

FMC   - Federal Maritime Commission

FRA   - Federal Railroad Administration, DOT

FSU   - Federal Soviet Union

GAO   - General Accounting Office

GCRT   - Greater Cleveland Regional Transit Authority

GDP   - Gross Domestic Product

GICW   - Gulf Intracoastral Authority Waterway

GPS   - Global Positioning System

HAZMAT   - Hazardous Materials

HE   - High Explosive

HERF   - High Energy Radio Frequency

HPM   - High Power Microwaves

IAP   - Infrastructure Assurance Program

ICC   - Incident Command Centers

ICTF   - Intermodal Container Transfer Facility

IMB   - International Maritime Bureau

IMO   - International Maritime Organization

INS   - Immigration and Naturalization Service

IRA   - Irish Republican Army

IS   - Information System Network

ISO   - International Standard Organization

ISTEA   - Intermodal Surface Transportation Efficiently Act

IT   - Island Transit

ITS	- Intelligent Transportation System
JPO	- Joint Program Office
KAPP	- Key Asset Protection Program
LACMTA	- Los Angeles County Metropolitan Transportation Authority
LASH	- Lighter Aboard Ship
LAW	- Light Anti-tank Weapons
MATA	- Memphis Area Transit Authority
MARTA	- Metropolitan Atlanta Rapid Transit Authority
MAW	- Medium Anti-tank Weapons
MBTA	- Massachusetts Bay Transportation Authority
MNLF	- Moro National Liberation Front
MSC	- Military Sealift Command
MTA	- Maryland Mass Transit Administration
NAS	- National Academy of Sciences; or National Airspace System
NBI	- National Bridge Inventory
NCSC	- National Cargo Security Council
NDTA	- National Defense Transportation Association
NFTA	- Niagara Frontier Transportation Authority
NHS	- National Highway System
NISC	- National Information Security Committee
NSTAC	- National Security Telecommunication Advisory Committee, President
NSTC	- National Science and Technology Committee's
NSWC	- Naval Surface Warfare Center
NYCT	- New York City Transit
OIS	- Office of Intelligence and Security
OTS	- Office of Transportation Security
PA	- Port Authority
PATCO	- Port Authority Transit Corporation
PCCIP	- President's Commission on Critical Infrastructure Protection
PHS	- Public Health Service, DHHS
P.L.	- Public Law
PLC	- Programmable Login Controls
PONTIS	- (Latin for "Bridge")
PWSA	- Ports and Waterways Safety Act

RDD   - Radiological Dispersion Device

RO-RO   - Roll-On-Roll-Off

RSPA   - Research and Special Programs Administration

RTD   - Regional Transportation District

RTG   - Rubber Tired Gantry

SCADA   - Supervisory Control And Data Acquisition System

SCCTD   - Santa Clara County Transportation District

SDTI   - San Diego Trolley, Inc.

SDV   - Swimmer Delivery Vehicles

SEPTA   - Southeastern Pennsylvania Transportation Authority

SOF   - Special Operation Force

SRTD   - Sacramento Regional Transit District

STRAHNET   - Strategic Highway Corridor Network

TMC   - Traffic Management Centers

TOFC   - Trailer-On-Flat-Car

UN   - United Nation

UPS   - United Parcel Service

USCG   - United Stated Coast Guard

VAP   - Vulnerability Assessment Program

VMS   - Variable Message Sings

VNTSC   - Volpe National Transportation System Center

WMATA   - Washington Metropolitan Area Transit Authority

WMD   - Weapons of Mass Destruction or Disruption

APPENDIX D - BIBLIOGRAPHY

1. "High Tech Cargo Theft," A Presentation at the US Capitol, MaryLu Korkuch, Executive Director, Technology Theft Prevention Foundation, April 9, 1996.
2. "Fraud, Hijacking and Theft of Valuables," Patrick Barco, Chair, Container Security, Canadian Bureau of Marine Underwriters, www.webcom.com/cbmu
3. "Railroad Infrastructure Vulnerability: Signaling and Control Systems (working papers)," Gertler, J. and Allen, D., 1998.
4. *A Force on the Move: The Story of the British Transport Police, 1825-1995*, Images Publishing (Malvern) Ltd., Worcestershire, England, 1995.
5. AAR Railroad Facts, 1997 Edition, L.C. Carel, No. A66-7305, September 1997.
6. Albert O'Leary. "Super Cops of the Subway," *Transit Policing* Vol. 3 n. 1, Winter/Spring 1993.
7. Barry M. Tarnef quoted in "Security of U.S. Ports challenged by Thieves, Smugglers, and Terrorists" by Carlos J. Salzano in *Traffic World* (25 September 1989).
8. Beier, Church, Frey and Zebe, "Flow of Selected Hazardous Materials by Rail," US DOT, DOT-VNTSC-RSPA-90-1, May 1991.
9. Boyd Maier & Associates, "Public Transportation Vulnerability to Terrorism and Acts of Extreme Violence," January 1998.
10. Boyd Maier, "Criminal Use of the Transportation Infrastructure," October 27, 1997.
11. Boyd Maier, "Effects of Aging Infrastructure on Transportation."
12. Boyd, Annabelle and Sullivan, John P., 1997. "Emergency Preparedness for Transit Terrorism," *Synthesis of Transit Practice 27,* National Academy Press, Washington D.C., pp. 18-19.
13. Boyd, M. Annabelle and Maier, M. Patricia. State Safety Oversight Security Handbook, USDOT, FTA, 1997.
14. Boyd, Maier & Associates, Inc. "Addressing Events-Related Violence," *Transit Policing,* Vol. 5 n. 1, Fall 1995.
15. Boyd, Maier & Associates, Inc. 1997. *Critical Incident Management Guidelines.*
16. Clarke, Ronald V. Preventing Mass Transit Crime, Vol. 6. Criminal Justice Press, New York, 1996.
17. Closeup Foundation, "Domestic Terrorism," http://closeup.org/terror, January 1997.
18. Cooper and Munley, "Bridge Research, Leading the Way to the Future," http://www.tfhrc.gov/pubrds/summer95/p95su23.
19. Daniels, Ressler and Fisher, "Vulnerability Assessment and Ranking of Steel Bridges," Transportation Research Record 1290, Volume 1, Third Bridge Engineering Conference, March 10, 1991.
20. Dinning, Micheal G., "Technology and Innovation in Transit Security," *Transit Policing,* Vol. 7, n. 1 Spring 1997.
21. Maio, Dominic and Liu,Tai-Kuo, "Truck Transportation of Hazardous Materials," DOT, DOR-TCS-RSPA-87-8, December 1987.
22. Donohue, Kenneth J. *Terrorism: Real Life Experiences, The American Perspective*, FTA, 1996.
23. Ed Tagliaferri, "Companies, Family Settle Lawsuit in I287 Blast," Gannett Suburban Newspapers http://www.nynews.com/archive/me60827d.

24. Edward V. Badolato, National Cargo Security Council, "The Current Cargo Crime Situation: A Presentation at the U.S. Capitol," April 9, 1996.
25. Eve Hinman, "Approach for Designing Civilian Structures Against Terrorist Attack," http://www.fail.com/feature/article2.
26. Failure Analysis Associates, "The Bombing of the Oklahoma City Federal Building: A Failure Analysis," 1996, http://www.fail.com/feature/article3.
27. Federal Highway Administration, "Prevention and Control of Highway Tunnel Fires," Report No. FHWA/RD-83/032, May 1984.
28. Federal Highway Administration, "The Status of the Nation's Highway Bridge: Highway Bridge Replacement and Rehabilitation Program and National Bridge Inventory," Thirteenth Report to Congress, May 1997.
29. Federal Highway Administration, "Recording and Coding Guide for the Structure Inventory and Appraisal of the Nation's Bridges," FHWA-ED-89-044, December 1988.
30. Foster-Miller Inc., "Railroad Infrastructure Vulnerability: Bridge and Tunnel," December 1997.
31. Massingham, G., "Terrorism: Assessing the Threat," Dispatch, Volume VII, Number 1, Spring 1997.
32. General Accounting Office. "Combating Terrorism, Status of DoD Efforts to Protect Its Forces Overseas," GAO/NSIAD-97-207, July 1997.
33. General Accounting Office, "Bridge Infrastructure: Matching the Resources to the Need," GAO/RCED-91-167, July 1991.
34. Greenwood, "A Relative Assessment of Putative Biological-Warfare Agents," Lincoln Laboratory Technical Report 1040, July 17, 1997.
35. DeGeneste, Henry I. and. Sullivan, John P, *Policing Transportation Facilities*, Charles C. Thomas, Springfield, Illinois, 1994.
36. http://www.dot.fra.gov.
37. Inside ITS, "ITS Systems Help Steer Travelers Around Collapsed Bridge In New York," Inside ITS, Vol. 17, No 22, November 17, 1997.
38. Muller, Gerhardt, "Intermodal Freight Transportation," 3rd Edition,
39. James Broder, "Risk Analysis and the Security Survey," Butterworth Publishers, 1984.
40. Kaufmann, Meltzer and Schmid, "The Economic Impact of a Bioterrorist Attack: Are Prevention and Post Attack Intervention Programs Justifable," http://www.cdc.gov/ncidod/EID/Vol3, No2.
41. Luchian F. Sergiu, "Memorial Tunnel Fire Test Program," TR News 190, May-June 1997.
42. Mayer, "The Biological Weapon: A Poor Nation's Weapon of Mass Destruction," http://www.cdsar.af.mil/battle.
43. Morelli, Thomas D., "DataBase of Containerized Maritime Cargo Theft Incidents: A Strategic Tool for Reducing Vulnerability," U.S. Department of Transportation (Washington, D.C.).
44. Newsletter, "Structural Engineers Combat Terrorism," Volume 9, Number 1, Spring 1996.
45. NOAA, "Oil and Hazardous Substances Planning and Response Considerations," June 1990.
46. Norman Y. Mineta International Institute for Surface Transportation Policy Studies, 1991. *Terrorism in Surface Transportation,* San Jose State University. Appendix A.
47. Obremski, Frank L. and Wendel, Charles. "Crisis Intervention for Mass Transit Systems," *Transit Policing,* Vol. 4 n. 2, Fall 1994.
48. Oxley, J.C. "Non-Traditional Explosives: Potential Detection Problems" *Terrorism and Political Violence.* 5(2), p.30-47, 1993.
49. Policing Transportation Facilities
50. Pontis User's Manual, "Network Optimization System for Bridge Improvements and Maintenance," Federal Highway Administration.

51. Port of Baltimore web site, http://www.mpa.state.md.us/

52. Report by the Comptroller General of the United States, General Accounting Office, "Promotion of Cargo Security Receives Limited Support" (Washington, D.C., 1980).

53. Roth, Kathryn A. *San Francisco Bay Area Rapid Transit District Emergency Plan,* 1994.

54. Staff, "Editorial: Incident in White Plains," Transportation Topics, http://www.ttnews.com/weekly.archive/02.26.tw7.

55. Staff, "The Biological & Chemical Warfare Threat."

56. Stephen Sloan, "Terrorism: How Vulnerable is the United States?" http://www.terrorism.com/terrorist/sloan, May 1995.

57. Tagliaferri, "Companies, Family settle Lawsuit in I-287 Blast," Gannett Suburban Newspaper.

58. The Current Cargo Crime Situation, A Presentation at the US Capitol, Edward V. Badolato, National Cargo Security Council, Chairman

59. The Terrorist's Handbook, http://phoenix.phreebyrd.com.

60. Tom Gorman, "No One Hurt as Train Derails, but Rail Service is Disrupted." Los Angeles Times, February 24, 1996, A-17.

61. Train It! Volume IV, Number 24, 12/19/97.

62. Train It! Volume V, Number 3, 2/19/98.

63. Train It! Volume V, Number 4, 3/5/98.

64. Train It! Volume V, Number 5, 3/19/98.

65. Transportation Research Board, "Synthesis of Transit Practice 27: Emergency Preparedness for Transit Terrorism," 1997.

66. U.S. Coast Guard Navigation and Vessel Inspection Circular No. 3-96

67. U.S. Department of Transportation, Bureau of Transportation Statistics, *Transportation Statistics Annual Report,* 1995 (Washington, D.C.).

68. U.S. Department of Transportation, "A Report to the President on the National Cargo Security Program" (Washington, D.C), March 1980.

69. U.S. Department of Transportation Memorandum, "Departmental Guidance for the Valuation of Travel Time in Economic Analysis," Frank Kruesi, Assistant Secretary for Transportation Policy, April 9, 1997.

70. U.S. General Accounting Office, "Domestic Terrorism: Prevention Efforts in Selected Federal Courts and Mass Transit Systems," Washington, D.C., (GAO/PEMD-88-22), June 1988.

71. U.S. Information Agency, "Excerpts: FBI Report on Domestic Terrorism," April 1997, http://www.jya.com/fbi041797.

72. U.S. Information Agency, "Transcript: DoD on Emergency Plan/Domestic Terrorism," April 1997, http://www.jya.com/dod041697.

APPENDIX E – AUTHORITY OF THE SECRETARY OF TRANSPORTATION IN EMERGENCIES

The Secretary's Authority to Stop Transportation in Case of Threat

The Secretary has extensive authority to stop all air and water transportation; the Secretary has very little authority to stop any other mode of transportation.

The right to stop operation of a transportation system derives from one or more of three relationships. One, the owner has inherent authority to stop operation. Two, the operator has inherent authority to stop operation. Three, the Government – Federal, State, local, or tribal – can stop operation. Since the Federal Government is almost never the owner or operator of a civilian transportation system, the Federal Government has no inherent authority to stop operation and its authority is limited to what is conferred by statute or Executive Order, The Federal statutes and Executive Orders that confer authority on the Department of Transportation do not, except for air and water transportation, give DOT the authority to stop the operation of a transportation system unless we can show, with some specificity, that the system is operating in an unsafe manner.

Air. 49 USC 44701 – The Secretary, acting through the Federal Aviation Administration (FAA), may exclude all air traffic in a designated area of the United States, if needed for aviation safety or security, or national security. When TWA800 crashed, this is the authority that was used to keep all air traffic away from the crash site.) The Secretary can also, through FAA, order US-flag air carriers not to enter designated airspace of a foreign country as, for example, to keep airspace clear for rescue operations.

Water.

1. 50 USC 191 – Acting through the Coast Guard, the Secretary may regulate the movement of all foreign vessels in US waters; take possession of those vessels; and remove any of their officers, crew, and other persons not authorized by the Secretary to be aboard. (If the President declares a national emergency, the same actions may be taken against US-flag vessels.) Any exclusion zones that are established must be approved by the President.

2. 33 USC 1226 – To protect against terrorism, the Secretary, acting through the Coast Guard, may establish exclusion zones.

3. 33 USC 984 and 1226 – The Secretary, acting through the St. Lawrence Seaway Development Corporation, may stop traffic through those portions of the St. Lawrence Seaway subject to US jurisdiction, if needed for safety or security of the Seaway, or for national security; hence, no deepwater vessels could enter or leave the Seaway.

Private automobile / truck / bus. The Secretary possesses no authority to order all motor vehicles to stop operating, or to ban motor vehicle operations on any type of highway. With minor exceptions, highways in the US are not owned operated by the Department of Transportation, so the Secretary cannot exercise authority as their proprietor; arguably, the proprietor State or Federal agency could. The Secretary also does not possess regulatory authority to stop private motor vehicle transportation. Specific commercial motor vehicles can be ordered out of service on the showing that their operation is hazardous, but, at least conventionally, that requires a showing specific to each vehicle.

Commuter rail / bus. The Secretary possesses no authority to direct cessation of the operations of transit systems in the US; none of the statutes conveys this nor do the grant agreements with individual system operators. In fact, 49 USC 5324(c) specifically denies the Secretary the authority to regulate transit system operations; however, see *The Secretary's Authority to Marshal Transportation for Evacuation or Rescue in Case of Emergency*, below.

Inter-city rail: The Secretary possesses no authority to order a railroad to cease operating for any reason other than safety problems with that railroad. However, the Surface Transportation Board can order railroads not to operate in a designated area of the US.

Special Coast Guard Authority. 14 USC 141 – The Secretary, acting through the Coast Guard and its auxiliary, has extraordinary authority to assist any federal, State, or local agency in any way in which the Coast Guard is especially qualified, and that authority is not limited to water transportation. Examples: If the President prohibits travel across an international boundary, the Secretary may assist in preventing that travel; and the Secretary may provide aerial surveillance and rescue, armed security, and other services for which the Coast Guard is specially qualified.

The Secretary's Authority to Marshal Transportation for Evacuation or Rescue in Case of Emergency

The Secretary has extensive authority in all modes of transportation; in fact, the Secretary has more authority to organize transportation in case of an emergency than to suspend that transportation in the same emergency. Under the Defense Production Act and related authorities, the President (delegated to the Secretary for air and motor vehicle (truck and bus) transportation, and transit) can issue orders to carriers to provide transportation designated areas, if needed to relieve an emergency situation. (Example: the Secretary can order transit operators in the affected area to evacuate all persons threatened by a hazardous material spill.) The Secretary has direct authority for water transportation under Coast Guard and Maritime Administration-administered laws; The Surface Transportation Board has authority for rail carriers. Hence, in case of an emergency that necessitates bringing personnel or supplies into an area, or evacuating the populace, the Secretary can provide a great deal of support.

Additional Government Authority in Time of War

In time of war, the President, acting through the Secretary of Defense, can take control of all or any part of the transportation system of the United States for the purpose of dealing with the emergency.

The authority is found in 10 USC 2644; it applies only in time of war. It was used during and after World War II, and during the Korean War, to take control of some railroads and transit systems.